Contents

Preface

Projects to Enrich School Mathematics (former title: *Student Merit Awards*) is a series of challenging research projects that provides enrichment material in a convenient format. In general, Level 1 is directed to upper elementary school students, Level 2 to middle school, and Level 3 to secondary school. The topics either are not found in the standard curriculum or represent a more in-depth study of standard topics. Most of the units contain material familiar to many teachers—material they would like to include in lessons but for which they never seem to have the time.

Teachers can either assign units to be done or allow students to select those that interest them. Care should be taken to match topics with the student's mathematical maturity. Units vary in length; most require between ten and thirty hours of outside research and writing. Many of the references can be found in school libraries and some in public or nearby college libraries. Students may occasionally need to consult people from the community or nearby colleges for information. Teachers should require students to credit their sources of information.

Each unit is composed of largely independent projects to be completed. A "guide" following many projects furnishes some essential information or hints and may also include drawings to present crucial information. The references are listed near the end of the unit. Many of the units include ideas for further investigations. These are meant to be motivational and may or may not be required by the teacher.

The material has been put into reproducible form for student use. The teacher notes for each unit include key information and solutions when appropriate. This section should be kept secure from the students.

This program was originally organized with the cooperation of five affiliated groups. Thanks go to the following representatives, who helped to acquire authors.

Jennifer Smith, Missouri Council of Teachers of Mathematics
Shirley Przybylski, Illinois Council of Teachers of Mathematics
Gloria Donaldson, Alabama Council of Teachers of Mathematics
J. Paul McLaughlin, Northern Indiana Council of Teachers of Mathematics
Patsy Johnson, Texas Council of Teachers of Mathematics

Special thanks go to Jane Martin and Richard Lodholz for the long hours spent in reviewing and helping to edit the manuscript. Without their help and advice, this book would not have been finished.

Applications of the Microcomputer in Mathematics

HUGH IMBODEN

MICROCOMPUTERS have become a familiar part of our culture. They are found in homes, businesses, factories, doctors' and lawyers' offices, scientific laboratories, schools, and many other places. They are used for a wide variety of applications. People who can create programs to accomplish specific tasks with the computer are in great demand. The power of the computer is awesome, but that power can be fully realized only through the creation and use of equally powerful programs. Learning to use a microcomputer is fun. The real fun and the real challenge, however, is in learning to write programs that make use of the fantastic speed and computational power of the computer. The purpose of your work in this topic area is to introduce you to some applications for the microcomputer and to encourage you to produce programs in areas in which the computer is an especially valuable tool.

A note to the programmer: Two things are desirable in completed programs. One is that the program does what it is intended to do. The other is that the program should be *accessible* to the user—that is, when the user runs the program, it should be clear what the program is intended to do and what the user is expected to do. The program should anticipate responses by the user and provide suitable reactions so that the program will continue to run correctly even though the user may supply incorrect or extraneous data. Make your programs "user friendly" at every turn. Use plenty of REM statements to let others who read your programs know what you intended and how you intended to accomplish it.

Projects

Project 1

Read about Newton's method for approximating roots of polynomial equations. Then do the following:

1. Write a program in BASIC to calculate a root of $y = x^4 + 3x^3 - 4x^2 - 1$. Calculate the root in the interval between 1 and 2 to the nearest 0.0001.

2. Write a program in BASIC so that the user can enter a polynomial equation and its first derivative along with a first estimate of the root. The program should calculate the root so it is correct to some specified degree of accuracy and then print the value of the root.

Guide: Reference 1 will help you learn about Newton's method (sometimes referred to as Newton-Raphson iteration). Any book on the theory of equations will have a fairly extensive section on this, but remember that you need to know only enough to use Newton's method on a polynomial equation. You don't really need to understand everything about this method and about derivatives in order to use the formula for the purposes of this program.

Although it is possible to write a program so that the first derivative of a polynomial function is found by computer, you may write these programs so that the derivative is entered by the user.

Project 2

1. Read your microcomputer manual to learn which special functions it has. These are usually called *built-in* or *intrinsic* functions. Write a paper showing each of these functions as well as a description of the function in your own words and at least one example showing what it does.

Guide: Built-in functions are very important because they make the job of writing programs much easier. For instance, without the square root function, SQR(X), each time we needed to find or use the square root of a number we would need to write a part of the program to find the root. With the built-in function, the computer furnishes the root of X when we write SQR(X).

In writing your paper use a form like this:

LOG(X) returns the natural logarithm of the argument X.

Example: LOG(1) = 0, LOG(5) = 1.6094

2. Read about *defined functions* and write a paper telling why it would be helpful to have this feature on your microcomputer. To complete this project, rewrite the program 1 in Project 1 using defined functions.

Guide: Your microcomputer manual might have information on defined functions. In any event, you can find out about them in Reference 5. There is a significant difference between writing functions in a program in the form $Y = 3*X^2 + 2*X - 7$ and writing them in the form $FNA(X) = 3*X^2 + 2*X - 7$. Be sure you understand this difference as it applies to writing programs.

Project 3

Read about *subroutines* (sometimes called *subprograms*). Be sure you understand how to send control of a program in BASIC to a subroutine and how to get back to the proper place in the main program. Make certain you understand why subroutines are considered to be so important. Use subroutines to write a program to accept data about a triangle and, if possible, to find the area of that triangle.

Guide: Your microcomputer manual should provide a great deal of information on subroutines. To complete the project, you should consider this question: Why put part of the program in a subroutine? Why not just include it in the main body of the program? In other words, you are to decide and report on what advantage there might be in writing programs that make use of subroutines. Reference 4 offers some interesting ideas on this subject.

As you begin to write your program, recall these three ways to find the area of a triangle:

1. $A = 1/2\ bh$
2. $A = 1/2\ ab * \sin C$
3. $A = \sqrt{s(s - a)(s - b)(s - c)}$, where $s = (a + b + c)/2$.

Use these three methods as you plan and write your program. The program should ask for information about the sides and angles of a triangle and then branch to the appropriate subroutine for that set of data.

Project 4

Find out what a *matrix* is in mathematics and how to multiply matrices. Then write a program that will do these things:

- Allow the input of two numbers in a 1 × 2 matrix.
- Allow the input of four numbers in a 2 × 2 matrix.
- Multiply these two matrices in the order given above.
- Print the two matrices, the indicated product, and the product.

Guide: You certainly don't need to know everything there is to know about matrices to write this program—just what they are and how to multiply a 1 × 2 matrix by a 2 × 2 matrix. References 2 and 5 have sections on matrices, as do most advanced algebra textbooks.

Some computers that use BASIC have a special kind of built-in statement that allows matrices to be stored, manipulated, and printed. Check to see if your microcomputer has this capability. The BASIC statements would be MAT READ, MAT INPUT, MAT PRINT, and so on. If your microcomputer allows MAT statements, you may use them to check your calculations.

Further Investigations

As you were doing Project 4, you may have wondered if there is any practical use for something as strange looking as these matrices. In fact, there is one use that is particularly interesting and fairly easy to understand. You can find lots of information about Markov chains in Reference 3 and in several other books in your library. You can use a program like the one in Project 4 to solve problems involving Markov chains. Reference 6 has a particularly straightforward explanation of one use of Markov chains.

One of the beautiful things about computer programming is that you will never run out of new and exciting challenges. There are always new horizons to be explored. For example, a book on trigonometry can be a source of interesting problems that can be solved on the computer. Creating programs to compute unknown sides or angles of triangles using the law of sines or the law of cosines is just one possibility.

REFERENCES

1. Dolciani, Mary, Edwin F. Beckenbach, Alfred J. Donnelly, Ray C. Jurgensen, and William Wooton. *Modern Introductory Analysis.* Boston: Houghton Mifflin Co., 1974.
2. Golden, Neal. *Computer Programming in the BASIC Language.* New York: Harcourt Brace Jovanovich, 1981.
3. Kemeny, John, and Thomas Kurtz. *BASIC Programming.* New York: John Wiley & Sons, 1971.
4. Nagin, Paul, and Henrey Ledgard. *BASIC with Style.* Rochelle Park, N.J.: Hayden Book Co., 1978.
5. Peckham, Herbert. *BASIC: A Hands-on Method.* New York: McGraw-Hill Book Co., 1978.
6. Croft Teacher's Service. "An Introduction to Markov Chains." In *Model for Teaching: Senior High School Mathematics."* New London, Conn.: Croft Educational Services, 1972.

Teacher Notes

Project 1

The formula required here is

$$x_1 = x_0 - \frac{f(x_0)}{f'(x_0)} \ .$$

In part 1 the student will have to learn how to find the first derivative of a polynomial function. The program is then as follows:

```
10      REM: THIS PROGRAM WILL COMPUTE THE ROOT OF A POLYNOMIAL
20      REM: FUNCTION TO ANY DESIRED DEGREE OF ACCURACY.
30      REM: IT MAKES USE OF THE NEWTOM-RAPHSON ITERATION
40      REM: METHOD (SOMETIMES CALLED NEWTON'S METHOD).
50      REM:
60      REM: THE FUNCTION IS HERE GIVEN ALONG WITH THE FIRST
70      REM: DERIVATIVE AND THE DESIRED DEGREE OF ACCURACY
80      REM:
90      REM: CLEAR THE SCREEN AND HOME THE CURSOR
100 CLS
110      REM: CALL FOR THE INITIAL VALUE OF X
120 INPUT "TYPE IN THE VALUE AT WHICH YOU WANT ITERATION TO BEGIN";X
130      REM: EVALUATE THE FUNCTION FOR THE CURRENT VALUE OF X
140 LET F=X↑4+3*X↑3-4*X↑2-1
150      REM: EVALUATE THE FIRST DERIVATIVE FOR THE CURRENT
160      REM: VALUE OF X
170 LET F1=4*X↑3+9*X↑2-8*X
180      REM: CHECK THE VALUE OF THE DERIVATIVE
190 IF F1=0 PRINT "F'(X)=0 FOR THIS VALUE OF X. CHOOSE ANOTHER":GOTO120
200      REM: EVALUATE THE QUOTIENT F(X)/F'(X)
210 LET Q=F/F1
220      REM: SAVE THE CURRENT VALUE OF X IN VARIABLE 'Y'
230 Y=X
240      REM: PRINT THE CURRENT VALUE OF X
250 PRINT Y
260      REM: CALCULATE THE NEW VALUE OF X
270 LET X=X-Q
280      REM: CHECK TO SEE IF THE CURRENT VALUE OF X IS
290      REM: IN THE CORRECT RANGE
300 IF ABS(X-Y)>=.0001 THEN 140
310 PRINT "THE REQUIRED ROOT: X IS APPROXIMATELY";X
320 END
```

The idea behind the question in part 2 is to make the program more useful and to suggest that the student explore some different ways of writing interactive programs. In order to make the program simpler to write, it might be a good idea to suggest the "trick" of asking the user to supply some lines of the program. This requires a bit of doing, but it is easier than asking for the degree of the function, the values of the coefficients, and so on. Below is a list of what should become a subroutine for this purpose.

```
10   CLS
20   PRINT"PLEASE FOLLOW THESE INSTRUCTIONS CAREFULLY. THE"
30   PRINT"PROGRAM WILL NOT RUN CORRECTLY UNLESS YOU DO EXACTLY"
40   PRINT"AS I SAY . . ."
50   PRINT"WHEN YOU SEE THE READY AT THE BOTTOM OF THE SCREEN,"
60   PRINT"TYPE IN THE FOLLOWING . . . THE LINE NUMBER 150"
70   PRINT"FOLLOWED BY THE FUNCTION SOLVED FOR Y . . . PRESS ENTER . . ."
80   PRINT"THEN THE LINE NUMBER 160 FOLLOWED BY THE DERIVATIVE OF"
90   PRINT"THE FUNCTION SOLVED FOR Y1 . . . PRESS ENTER . . . FOR EXAMPLE"
100  PRINT"150 Y=3*X↑2+2*X-5"
110  PRINT"160 Y1=6*X+2"
120  PRINT". . . THEN TYPE IN RUN 140 AND PRESS ENTER."
130  END
140  INPUT"ENTER YOUR FIRST ESTIMATE OF THE ROOT";X
170  Z=X
180  X=X-Y/Y1: IF ABS(Z-X)<.0001 PRINT"THE ROOT IS APPROXIMATELY";X:END
190  GOTO 150
```

Project 2

Each microcomputer has its own set of built-in functions (sometimes called *intrinsic* functions). Make sure that the student gets the main idea behind each one. The completed paper for this project should include—

- the list of built-in functions;
- a discussion on defined functions;
- the rewritten form of program 1 from Project 1.

A list of one possible program follows.

```
10      REM THIS PROGRAM WILL COMPUTE THE ROOT OF A POLYNOMIAL
20      REM FUNCTION TO ANY DESIRED DEGREE OF ACCURACY.
30      REM IT MAKES USE OF THE NEWTON-RAPHSON ITERATION
40      REM METHOD (SOMETIMES CALLED NEWTON'S METHOD).
50      REM
60      REM THE FUNCTION IS HERE GIVEN ALONG WITH THE FIRST
70      REM DERIVATIVE AND THE DESIRED DEGREE OF ACCURACY
80      REM
90      REM CLEAR THE SCREEN AND HOME THE CURSOR
100     REM
110 CLS
120     REM
130     REM DEFINE THE FUNCTION F(X)
140     REM
150 DEF FNA(X)=X↑4+3*X↑3−4*X↑2−1
160     REM
170     REM DEFINE THE FIRST DERIVATIVE FUNCTION F'(X)
180     REM
190 DEF FND(X)=4*X↑3+9*X↑2−8*X
200     REM
210     REM INPUT THE X(0)
220     REM
230 INPUT"PLEASE TYPE IN THE POINT ON THE X-AXIS AT WHICH
I SHOULD BEGIN THE ITERATION PROCESS";X
240     REM
250     REM SAVE THE CURRENT VALUE OF X IN 'Y' FOR LATER
260     REM COMPARISON WITH THE NEW VALUE OF X
270     REM
280 Y=X
290     REM
300     REM PRINT THE CURRENT VALUE OF X
310     REM OF ITERATION
320     REM
330 PRINTX
340     REM
350     REM CALCULATE THE NEW VALUE OF X
360     REM
370 X=X−FNA(X)/FND(X)
380     REM
390     REM CHECK TO SEE IF THE VALUE OF X IS IN
400     REM THE DESIRED ACCURACY RANGE
410     REM
420 IFABS(Y−X)>=.0001GOTO280
430     REM
440     REM PRINT THE CURRENT VALUE OF X
450     REM
460 PRINTX
470 END
```

Project 3

The program listing should look something like the one that follows.

```
10   CLS
20   PRINT"THIS PROGRAM IS DESIGNED TO ACCEPT DATA ABOUT"
30   PRINT"A TRIANGLE AND, IF SUFFICIENT DATA IS GIVEN,"
40   PRINT"CALCULATE THE AREA OF THE TRIANGLE."
50   PRINT" "
60   PRINT"PLEASE TELL ME WHICH OF THE FOLLOWING BEST DESCRIBES "
70   PRINT"THE INFORMATION YOU HAVE ABOUT THIS TRIANGLE."
80   PRINT" "
90   PRINT"IF YOU KNOW A SIDE AND THE ASSOCIATED ALTITUDE      TYPE 1"
100  PRINT"IF YOU KNOW TWO SIDES AND THE INCLUDED ANGLE       TYPE 2"
110  PRINT"IF YOU KNOW THREE SIDES OF THE TRIANGLE            TYPE 3"
120  PRINT"IF YOU DO NOT KNOW ANY OF THESE                    TYPE 4"
130  INPUT "TYPE 1, 2, 3 OR 4";A
140  CLS
150  ON A GOSUB 260,310,400,480
160  IF A=4 THEN 180
170  PRINT"THE AREA OF THE TRIANGLE IS";AR
180  INPUT"DO YOU HAVE ANOTHER . . . TYPE Y FOR YES, N FOR NO";A$
190  CLS
200  IF A$="Y" GOTO 50
210  CLS
220  PRINTCHR$(23)"SO LONG FROM YOUR DELUXE COMPUTER AREA FINDER"
230  FOR Z=1TO4000:NEXT
240  END
250     REM:  THE SUBROUTINE FOR TYPE 1
260  INPUT"PLEASE TYPE IN THE LENGTH OF THE KNOWN SIDE";AA
270  INPUT"PLEASE TYPE IN THE LENGTH OF THE ALTITUDE";BB
280  AR=.5*AA*BB
290  RETURN
300     REM:  THE SUBROUTINE FOR TYPE 2
310  INPUT"TYPE THE LENGTH OF ONE SIDE";CC
320  INPUT"TYPE THE LENGTH OF THE OTHER SIDE";DD
330  INPUT"PLEASE INDICATE WHETHER THE MEASURE OF THE ANGLE
IS IN RADIANS OR DEGREES . . .TYPE R OR D";ZZ$
340  IFZZ$<>"R" AND ZZ$<>"D" THEN 330
350  INPUT"PLEASE TYPE THE MEASURE OF THE . . INCLUDED . . ANGLE";EE
360  IF ZZ$="D" THEN EE=EE*3.14159/180
370  IF EE>=3.14159 THEN PRINT:PRINT"EACH OF THE ANGLES OF A TRIANGLE MUST BE LESS THAN PI
     RADIANS OR 180 DEGREES. CHECK YOUR ANGLE SIZE AGAIN, PLEASE.":PRINT:GOTO350
375  AR=.5*CC*DD*SIN(EE)
380  RETURN
390     REM:  THE SUBROUTINE FOR TYPE 3
400  INPUT"TYPE THE MEASURE OF THE SHORTEST SIDE OF THE TRIANGLE";FF
410  INPUT"TYPE THE MEASURE OF THE NEXT SHORTEST SIDE";GG
420  INPUT"TYPE THE MEASURE OF THE LONGEST SIDE";HH
421  IF FF>GG OR FF>HH OR GG>HH GOTO400
425  IF FF+GG<=HH PRINT"ACCORDING TO THE TRIANGLE INEQUALITY THIS IS NOT A TRIANG
     LE":GOTO180
430  S=(FF+GG+HH)*.5
440  T=S*(S-FF)*(S-GG)*(S-HH)
450  AR=SQR(T)
460  RETURN
470     REM:  THE 'COP-OUT' FOR THE REST
480  PRINT"I'M SORRY, YOU'VE GOT TO DO THIS ONE ON YOUR OWN."
490  PRINT"  "
500  RETURN
```

Project 4

You will need to check to see that the student is finding out how to multiply matrices. References 2 and 5 and many microcomputer manuals have information on writing subroutines to accept matrices without using the MAT statements. Listed below are some subroutines that will allow input, multiplication, and printing (patterned after a similar listing in Radio Shack's *Level II BASIC Reference Manual* [Fort Worth, Tex.: Radio Shack, 1979], pages 6/4–6/7). If the student has difficulty with this project, use this information sparingly. The idea is to persuade the student to create the program.

```
1000  REM:  1X2 MATRIX INPUT SUBROUTINE
1010  PRINT "INPUT ROW";1
1020  FOR J=1 TO 2
1030  INPUT A(1,J)
1040  NEXT J
1050  RETURN

2000  REM:  2X2 MATRIX INPUT SUBROUTINE
2010  FOR I=1 TO 2
2020  PRINT "INPUT ROW";I
2030  FOR J= 1 TO 2
2040  INPUT B(I,J)
2050  NEXT J,I
2060  RETURN

3000  REM:  MATRIX MULTIPLICATION SUBROUTINE
3010  FOR J=1 TO 2
3020  C(1,J) = 0
3030  FOR K = 1 TO 2
3040  C(1,J) = C(1,J) + A(1,K) * B(K,J)
3050  NEXT K
3060  NEXT J
3070  RETURN

4000  REM: 1X2 MATRIX PRINT SUBROUTINE
4010  FOR J= 1 TO 2
4020  PRINT A(1,J),
4030  NEXT J: PRINT
4040  RETURN

5000  REM: 2X2 MATRIX PRINT SUBROUTINE
5010  FOR I = 1 TO 2
5020  FOR J =1 TO 2
5030  PRINT B(I,J),
5040  NEXT J: PRINT
5050  NEXT I: PRINT
5060  RETURN

6000  REM: PRODUCT MATRIX PRINT SUBROUTINE
6010  FOR J = 1 TO 2
6020  PRINT C(1,J),
6030  NEXT J: PRINT
6040  RETURN
```

The Fourth Dimension and Beyond

ROBERTA SIMONSON

WE live in a three-dimensional world. It is easy for you to visualize a block when a cube is mentioned or a ball when a sphere is mentioned. But suppose you were a two-dimensional being—how would a cube or a sphere look? Or how would you describe a four-dimensional cube or sphere? The object of the work you will be doing is to gain knowledge and visual concepts of dimensions other than those with which you are familiar.

Projects

Project 1

Write a definition of these terms used in n-dimensional geometry: Platonic solids, tetrahedron, cube, octahedron, icosahedron, dodecahedron, polyhedron, polytope, hypersphere, overcube, hyperhypercube, tesseract, cuboid, hypersolid, and n-space.

Guide: The prime reason for defining these terms is that they are not usually found in a regular dictionary. References 6, 8, and 9 will help you find them. You will not find them precisely defined in each case but may have to piece the definitions together. You will also get some idea of the general meaning of n-dimensional geometry while reading these references.

Project 2

Explain in a paragraph how a two-dimensional being would see an object like a sphere. In a second paragraph, speculate on how you would see a hypersphere.

Guide: In References 1 and 2, you will find the answer to the first part of this requirement. The two books are very short and easy to read. As you read other references, you will find that many of them refer to Reference 1; it has become a base for thinking in other dimensions. In fact, it has become so popular that you may have already read it.

Reference 8 describes in detail how to picture a hypersphere. Now, in your own words, what would you see?

Project 3

Develop formulas for coordinate geometry in n-space for the following: distance between two points; equation of a plane; equation of a sphere; Euler's formula.

Guide: In two-dimensional space, a distance formula is $(x_2 - x_1)^2 + (y_2 - y_1)^2 = d^2$. In three-dimensional space this becomes $(x_2 - x_1)^2 + (y_2 - y_1)^2 + (z_2 - z_1)^2 = d^2$. Now what would be a formula for distance in four-dimensional space? For five-dimensional space?

Using the same reasoning, find an analogous equation of a hyperplane in four-dimensional space using the standard $ax + by + c = 0$ as the two-dimensional model.

An equation of a sphere is $x^2 + y^2 + z^2 = r^2$. What is an equation of a hypersphere? For a hyperhypersphere?

Euler's formula for a regular polyhedron is the number of vertices minus the number of edges plus the number of faces is equal to 2 ($v - e + f = 2$). To develop this for n-space, it would be easier to use only one letter as a variable with numerical subscripts, such as $x_0 - x_1 + x_2 - x_3 = 0$ for four-dimensional space, with x_0 = number of vertices (points), x_1 = number of edges (line segments), x_2 = number of faces (planes), and x_3 = number of three-dimensional space faces. Using this as a basis, develop a formula for n-space.

Project 4

1. Discover formulas for finding the surface area and the volume of a hypersphere.
2. Finish filling in the table below:

	Number of vertices	Edges	Faces	Solids	Hyper-solids	Hyperhyper-solids
Point	1	—	—	—	—	—
Line segment	2	1	—	—	—	—
Square	4	4	1	—	—	—
Cube						
Hypercube						
Hyperhypercube						

3. The five regular polyhedrons in three-dimensional space are called the Platonic solids. How many regular polytopes are there in four-dimensional space? In five-dimensional space?

Guide: In geometry, you have found that the formula for the circumference of a circle is $2\pi r$ and that the surface area of a sphere is $4\pi r^2$.

a) What is the hypersurface area of a hypersphere? (No, it is not $8\pi r^3$.) You can find the answer by using calculus. References 3, 6, 8, and 9 also give the answer as well as the derivations of the formulas.

b) There is a relationship in the expansion of the binomial $(2a + b)^n$ to the number of vertices and edges. The expression $(2a + b)^1$ represents a line segment, so there are two vertices and one edge. In a square, $(2a + b)^2 = 4a^2 + 4ab + b^2$, which gives four vertices, four edges, and one face. Fill in the table.

c) You will discover the answer to these questions and learn additional facts in References 3, 6, and 9.

Project 5

Make a model of a tesseract.

Guide: Descriptions of tesseracts made from different materials are given. Choose the one that best suits the materials you have available. A cube on paper is a three-dimensional object drawn in two-dimensional space. The model of the tesseract is a four-dimensional object made in three-dimensional space.

Tesseract 1: The dimensions of the tesseract in figure 1 were used because the Plexiglas from which it was made was a gift and was 8½ inches wide. Plexiglas is easy to use. Because the Plexiglas that was used for this model was ⅛ inch thick, compensations were made on four of the trapezoids: ¼ inch was taken from the large bases, making them 8¼ inches, and ¼ inch was taken from one side of the large squares, making that side 8¼ inches. You may have to compensate in the same way. A figure of the tesseract follows. Count the vertices, faces, and edges. Do they check? You will need the following pieces of Plexiglas:

    6 squares, 8½″ × 8½″
    6 squares, 4¼″ × 4¼″
    12 isosceles trapezoids, top base 4¼″,
        bottom base 8½″, and altitude 2⅘″

It is best to use plastic cement or a Plexiglas solvent and tape the pieces together until the cement dries. It is helpful to do the small cube first and let it dry before you put the rest together. The tesseract must be strong because your friends and classmates will be fascinated and many will handle it.

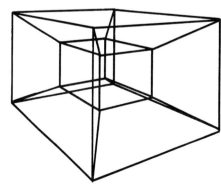

Fig. 1. Tesseract model

Tesseract 2: An alternative tesseract can be made from wire. Fourteen-gauge wire is easy to bend yet firm enough to hold its shape when the tesseract is finished. Wire coat hangers can also be used. The usual coat hanger has a straight portion of sixteen inches; so the outside cube can be made eight inches on edge. Pliers and wire cutters are needed.

Straighten four coat hangers, measure, and cut each into thirty-two-inch lengths. Make four squares eight inches on an edge to form the lateral faces of a cube. Tape the lateral edges together with plastic or cloth tape. The top and bottom are automatically there. If you wish to reinforce the top and bottom, you can make two more squares and tape one to the top and one to the bottom.

Cut sixteen-inch lengths to form squares, four inches on an edge. Make the four-inch cube as you did the eight-inch one.

Cut eight 4½-inch lengths of wire. Bend each end of the wires to form a hook, but leave 3⅕ inches of straight length in the middle. Attach one end of each wire to a vertex of the large cube and the other end to a vertex of the small cube. To keep the parts stationary, tape them in place. Now count the vertices, faces, and edges, and compare the count to the chart in Project 4.

REFERENCES

1. Abbot, Edwin. *Flatland—a Romance of Many Dimensions.* Reprint. New York: Dover Publications, 1960.
2. Burger, Dionys. *Sphereland—a Fantasy about Curved Spaces and an Expanding Universe.* Reprint. New York: Apollo Editions, 1969.
3. Coxeter, H. S. M. *Introduction to Geometry.* New York: John Wiley & Sons, 1969.
4. Hinton, Charles H. *Speculations on the Fourth Dimension.* Edited by Rudolf v. B. Rucker. New York: Dover Publications, 1980.
5. Kasner, Edward, and James Newman. *Mathematics and the Imagination.* New York: Simon & Schuster, 1940.
6. Manning, Henry P. *Geometry of Four Dimensions.* Reprint. New York: Dover Publications, 1956.
7. National Council of Teachers of Mathematics. *Multi-Sensory Aids in the Teaching of Mathematics.* Eighteenth Yearbook. Washington, D.C.: The Council, 1945.
8. Rucker, Rudolf v. B. *Geometry, Relativity and the Fourth Dimension.* New York: Dover Publications, 1977.
9. Sommerville, D. M. Y. *An Introduction to the Geometry of N-Dimensions.* 1929. Reprint. New York: Dover Publications, 1958.

Teacher Notes

The questions in the projects can be easily answered from the references. The student, when reading the references, will gain a great deal of additional information not asked for in this unit. The student will also be stimulated to look into related geometries. It is recommended that the following key be used only when the student has completed the projects so that the most information can be gained.

Project 1

- Platonic solids—the five regular convex solids of three-dimensional space: tetrahedron, cube, octahedron, dodecahedron, and icosahedron
- Tetrahedron—regular convex solid with four faces
- Cube—regular convex solid with six faces
- Octahedron—regular convex solid with eight faces
- Dodecahedron—regular convex solid with twelve faces
- Icosahedron—regular convex solid with twenty faces
- Polyhedron—finite convex region in three-dimensional space enclosed by planes
- Polytope—finite convex region in four-dimensional space enclosed by planes
- Hypersphere—spherical convex region in four-dimensional space
- Overcube—one of the names for a four-dimensional "cube"
- Hyperhypercube—"cube" in five-dimensional space
- Tesseract—perhaps the most common name of the "cube" in four-dimensional space
- Cuboid—another name for the "cube" in four-dimensional space
- Hypersolid—solid in four-dimensional space
- *N*-space—multidimensional space

Project 2

Because a two-dimensional being would see only in planes, as the sphere became visible, it would first be seen as a point. Then it would become a circle, which would become larger and larger until it reached the great circle, at which time it would begin decreasing in size until it was once again a point. A great circle is the circle formed when a plane intersects a sphere through the center of the sphere.

To a three-dimensional being, the hypersphere would appear as a point, then a partial sphere inflating in size until it reached the maximum diameter (at that time it would look like a sphere), then reducing in size until it became a point once again. It would then disappear from our three-dimensional space visibility.

Project 3

- Distance between two points:
- Four-dimensional space: $(x_2 - x_1)^2 + (y_2 - y_1)^2 + (w_2 - w_1)^2 = d^2$
- Five-dimensional space: $(x_2 - x_1)^2 + (y_2 - y_1)^2 + (w_2 - w_1)^2 + (v_2 - v_1)^2 = d^2$
  The variables w and v are optional; any other variables will also do.
- Equation of a plane: $ax + by + cz + d = 0$
  Equation of a hyperplane in four-dimensional space: $ax + by + cz + dw + e = 0$
- Equation of a hypersphere with center at origin and radius r: $x^2 + y^2 + z^2 + w^2 = r^2$
  Equation of a hyperhypersphere with center at origin and radius r: $x^2 + y^2 + z^2 + w^2 + v^2 = r^2$
- Euler's formula in n-space: $x_0 - x_1 + x_2 - x_3 + x_4 + \ldots + (-1)^{n-1}x_{n-1} = 1 + (-1)^{n-1}$

Project 4

1. The formula for the hypersurface of a hypersphere is $2\pi^2 r^3$. The formula for the hypervolume of a hypersphere is $\frac{1}{2}\pi^2 r^4$.

2. See table on next page.

3. In four-dimensional space, there are six regular convex polytopes. In five-dimensional space, there are only three regular polytopes. The student will find names given to some of these. Others are just referred to as 16-cell, 24-cell, and so on.

	Number of vertices	Edges	Faces	Solids	Hyper-solids	Hyperhyper-solids
Point	1	—	—	—	—	—
Line segment	2	1	—	—	—	—
Square	4	4	1	—	—	—
Cube	8	12	6	1	—	—
Hypercube	16	32	24	8	1	—
Hyperhypercube	32	80	80	40	10	1

Project 5

Making this model may seem to take too much time when scanning the directions. However, after gathering the materials, it can be done in less than four hours.

Tesseract 1: The student will put together the small cube, then while it is drying, two sets of four trapezoids each can be put together. These resemble frames when glued, or (to the highly imaginative person) lampshades. These can be glued to opposite faces of the small cube.

The problem of fitting arises when the trapezoids that are attached to the remaining edges of the cube are too large to fit, due to the thickness of the Plexiglas. The problem is solved if a trapezoid is made of cardboard to fit in this area and then the Plexiglas trapezoids trimmed to the shape of the cardboard model.

The large squares can now be glued to the large bases of each trapezoid. Once again, where the trapezoids have been trimmed, the large squares must also be trimmed.

Tesseract 2: The tesseract made from coat hangers requires more imagination than the Plexiglas model. It is also more difficult to make. If the materials must be bought, the coat hanger model is the cheaper of the two.

To get the corners acute, I placed the wire on a board and used the edge of the board for leverage. Electrical tape is best for taping the parts together. I tried liquid solder but it was not strong enough.

Another miniproject that is fascinating is a "bubble cube" made from flexible 24-gauge wire. I used a thirty-six-inch length of it and made a one-inch cube with a handle without cutting it. Six inches for the handle is laid off first, and then the wire is formed into one-inch segments until a cube is formed. You have to retrace your steps with the wire several times. It does not make any difference in the final project if some of the sides have been doubled. There will be a length at the end to twist back and forth to make the handle sturdy.

Dip the cube in a bubble solution. I used solution bought for children's bubble pipes. A model tesseract bubble is formed within the cube.

Finite Groups

ANDREA ROTHBART

I N THE year 2222, travelers from Earth discovered a society of intelligent beings on Titan. At first the Titans held the Earth people in disdain and refused to communicate with them. The breakthrough occurred when one of the astronauts observed a Titan rotating an equilateral triangle and then writing mathematical equations. The astronaut inquired into its meaning and was startled to hear this reply: "I'm investigating some examples of finite groups—in this case, the permutations of the vertices of an equilateral triangle. Have you dealt much with groups?"

The astronaut blushed. She recalled that her small son had read an article on finite groups in the intergalactic primer. Surely her planetmates had done extensive work in the theory of groups, but she herself had no knowledge of them.

"No, but if you would be kind enough to teach me . . ." she said.

Thereupon the Titan gave her the exercises that appear below. "If you diligently do as I direct," he said, "then you will learn what a finite group is and become familiar with several examples of this algebraic structure."

Project 1

Do the following exercises.

Exercise 1: Accurately draw an equilateral triangle on a piece of cardboard. Label the vertices 1, 2, and 3 both outside and inside the triangle. Write an *F* (for "Front") in the center of the triangle. (See fig. 1.) Cut out the triangle. Number the vertices on the back side of the triangle as follows: the vertex numbered 1 on the front should be numbered 1 on the back. Do the same with 2 and 3. Write a *B* in the center of the back side of the triangle. (See fig. 2.)

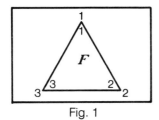

Fig. 1

Fig. 2

Exercise 2: There are six ways that you can fit the triangle into the hole in the cardboard. Can you find them?

Each time that you fit the triangle into the hole in the cardboard, you have, in effect, *permuted* the vertices of the triangle. These six permutations are functions from the set of vertices {1, 2, 3} of the triangle into itself.

Fit the triangle in the hole as it was before you cut it out. You have just mapped 1 to 1, 2 to 2, and 3 to 3. We will call this mapping *e*. Now rotate the triangle 120 degrees clockwise so that you are mapping 1 to 2, 2 to 3, and 3 to 1. We will call this mapping *f*.

Exercise 3: Another mapping has the effect of rotating the triangle 240 degrees clockwise. Which mapping is that? We will call this mapping *g*.

The function that maps 1 to 1, 2 to 3, and 3 to 2 can be effected by flipping the triangle over its vertical altitude. We call this mapping *h*.

Exercise 4: Let *i* represent the function that maps 1 to 3, 2 to 2, and 3 to 1. What physical motion corresponds to *i*? Let *j* represent the function that maps 1 to 2, 2 to 1, and 3 to 3. What physical motion corresponds to *j*?

Thus the functions *e*, *f*, and *g* can be thought of as clockwise rotations of 0, 120, and 240 degrees, respectively, whereas the functions *h*, *i*, and *j* can be thought of as flips of the triangle over its three altitudes. Practice these six permutations until you are comfortable with them by name.

Fit the triangle into its original position in the cardboard. Rotate the triangle 120 degrees clockwise (that is, do the mapping *f*). Now flip the triangle over its vertical altitude (that is, do the mapping *h*). When you have done so, you should have the situation shown in figure 3.

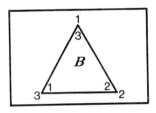

Fig. 3

Since *f* followed by *h* has the same effect as *i*, write *f* * *h* = *i*. Now, use your triangle to check that *j* * *i* = *f*; that *g* * *e* = *g*.

Exercise 5: Complete the following table:

*	e	f	g	h	i	j
e						
f					i	
g	g					
h						
i						
j					f	

Let *T* = {*e, f, g, h, i, j*}. Note that * is an operation on *T*. Furthermore, for any *a* in *T*, *a* * *e* = *a* and *e* * *a* = *a*. Since *e* has this property, it is called the * *identity in T.*

Note also that *f* * *g* = *e* and *g* * *f* = *e*. So *f* and *g* are called * *inverses in T.* What is the * inverse of *h*? (That is, what mapping *a* has the property that *a* * *h* = *e* and *h* * *a* = *e*?)

Exercise 6: Complete this table:

Function	e	f	g	h	i	j
*Inverse of function		g	f			

Exercise 7: It should be apparent from your answer to Exercise 5 that * is not a commutative operation. But is it an associative operation? Check several instances. (*Note.* If you wanted to prove that * was associative by checking every possible case, how many instances would you have to check? A far easier approach is to observe that * corresponds to function composition. Whenever *l, m, n* are any three functions from some set *S* onto itself, and *x* is an element of *S*, then ((*l* ∘ *m*) ∘ *n*) (*x*) = (*l* ∘ (*m* ∘ *n*)) (*x*).

Exercise 8: Compute ((*j* * *f*) * *g*) * *i*. (*Suggestion:* Since * is associative, ((*j* * *f*) * *g*) * *i* = (*j* * (*f* * *g*)) * *i* = (*j* * *e*) * *i* = *j* * *i*. Now look up *j* * *i* in your * table.)

Exercise 9: Compute the following. (Since * is associative, we can omit the parentheses.)

   a) $h * j * j * g * f * e * h$ b) $h * i * g * h * e * h$

To solve an equation over the rationals, such as ¾ x = ⅓, we might argue as follows:

What we write	**What we think**
3/4 x = 1/3	We will cleverly multiply both sides of the equation
so 4/3 · (3/4x) = 4/3 ·1/3	by 4/3, since 4/3 is the multiplicative inverse of 3/4.
so (4/3 · 3/4) · x = 4/3 · 1/3	Then, since multiplication is associative, we can
so 1 · x = 4/9	multiply the two fractions and get 1.
so x = 4/9	

The same kind of argument works in any system in which we have an associative operation, identity, and inverse. For example, to solve $f * x = i$ in $(T, *)$ we can argue as follows:

What we write	**What we think**
$f * x = i$	We will cleverly multiply both sides of the equation
so $g * (f * x) = i$	by g, since g is the inverse of f. Then, since * is
so $(g * f) * x = i$	associative, we can multiply g and f and get e.
so $e * x = i$	
so $x = i$	

Here is a slightly more complicated application of the same idea. Since * is an associative operation, we will leave out the parentheses.

To solve $h * x * g = f$, we argue:

$$h * x * g = f$$
so $\quad h * h * x * g = h * f$
so $\quad\quad e * x * g = h * f$
so $\quad\quad\quad\quad x * g = i$
so $\quad\quad\quad x * g * f = j * f$
so $\quad\quad\quad\quad x * e = j * f$
so $\quad\quad\quad\quad\quad x = i$

Check that $h * i * g$ is indeed f.

Exercise 10: Solve the following equations:

   a) $i * x * f = h$ b) $f * x * i = g$

Exercise 11: In Exercise 10b you should have obtained the answer h. What is wrong with the following argument?

$$f * x * j = g$$
so $\quad g * f * x * j = g * g$
so $\quad\quad e * x * j = f$
so $\quad\quad\quad\quad x * j = f$
so $\quad\quad\quad x * j * j = j * f$
so $\quad\quad\quad\quad x * e = j * f$
so $\quad\quad\quad\quad\quad x = i$

Observe that the properties of $(T, *)$ that allow us to routinely solve equations such as those in Exercise 10 are (a) associativity, (b) the existence of an identity, and (c) the existence of inverses.

Definition of a group: If S is a set and ∘ is an associative operation on S satisfying—

   a) there exists an element e of S such that for each a in S

   $\quad\quad a \circ e = a \quad\quad$ and $e \circ a = a$

   b) for each a in S, there exists b in S such that

   $\quad\quad a \circ b = e \quad\quad$ and $b \circ a = e$

then $(S, \circ)$ is called a *group*.

   The element e is called the ∘ identity of the group. Whenever $a \circ b = b \circ a = e$, then a and b are called ∘ inverses in s.

Problem: Suppose that $(S, \circ)$ is a group. Prove the following:

a) There is only one identity element in S. (*Hint:* Suppose there are two, e and e'. "Multiply" them together and see what you get.)

b) Each element of S has only one inverse. (*Hint:* Suppose that the element a has two inverses, b and c. Look at $c \circ (a \circ b)$.)

If $(S, \circ)$ is a group and S is a finite set, then $(S, \circ)$ is called a *finite group*. Thus, $(T, *)$ is an example of a finite group. In the following two problem sets, you will be introduced to two more examples of finite groups.

Project 2

You are probably familiar with clock arithmetic (modular 12 arithmetic) where, for example, $3 +_{12} 10 = 1$ and $2 \cdot_{12} 7 = 2$. Well, on Titan, clocks have seven hours, and so it seems more fitting to study modular 7 arithmetic here.

Let $Z_7 = \{0, 1, 2, 3, 4, 5, 6\}$. Define $\cdot_7$ as follows: For each a and b in Z_7, let $a \cdot_7 b$ be the remainder when ab is divided by 7. So, for example, $4 \cdot_7 3 = 5$, since 5 is the remainder when 12 is divided by 7.

Do the following exercises.

Exercise 1: Complete the following table:

$\cdot_7$	0	1	2	3	4	5	6
1							
2							
3							
4			5				
5							
6							

Unfortunately, $(Z_7, \cdot_7)$ is not a group, since 0 has no $\cdot_7$ inverse. So let's evict 0 from the set, leaving us $Z'_7 = \{1, 2, 3, 4, 5, 6\}$.

Exercise 2: By considering several instances, convince yourself that $\cdot_7$ is an associative operation on Z'_7. What is the identity element? Fill out the following table:

x	1	2	3	4	5	6
Inverse of x						

Thus $(Z'_7, \cdot_7)$ is another example of a finite group. That means we can solve certain types of equations rather routinely. But writing them can be tedious if we insist on using the subscripts on the operation signs. So, let's agree to omit the subscripts and simply write the words *mod 7* after any equation where all the multiplications are intended to be mod 7 multiplications.

To solve the equation $4 \cdot x \cdot 3 = 2$ mod 7, we can argue as follows:

$$4 \cdot x \cdot 3 = 2 \qquad \text{mod } 7$$
so $$2 \cdot 4 \cdot x \cdot 3 = 2 \cdot 2 \qquad \text{mod } 7$$
so $$1 \cdot x \cdot 3 = 2 \cdot 2 \qquad \text{mod } 7$$
so $$x \cdot 3 = 4 \qquad \text{mod } 7$$
so $$x \cdot 3 \cdot 5 = 4 \cdot 5 \qquad \text{mod } 7$$
so $$x \cdot 1 = 4 \cdot 5 \qquad \text{mod } 7$$
so $$x = 6$$

However, if we stop to observe that mod 7 multiplication is commutative, we realize that there is a shorter way to solve the equation:

$$4 \cdot x \cdot 3 = 2 \qquad \mathrm{mod}\ 7$$
so $\quad 3 \cdot 4 \cdot x = 2 \qquad \mathrm{mod}\ 7$ Since mod 7 multiplication is both
so $\quad\quad\ 5 \cdot x = 2 \qquad \mathrm{mod}\ 7$ commutative and associative
so $\quad 3 \cdot 5 \cdot x = 3 \cdot 2 \quad \mathrm{mod}\ 7$
so $\quad\quad\quad\ x = 6$

Exercise 3: Solve the following equations:

    a) $2 \cdot x \cdot 5 \cdot 4 = 3 \bmod 7$ b) $3 \cdot 5 \cdot x \cdot 2 \cdot 3 = 1 \bmod 7$

If you have been bemoaning the eviction of 0, we can reinstate it and still have a group by adding mod 7 rather than multiplying.

Exercise 4: Let $Z_7 = \{0, 1, 2, 3, 4, 5, 6\}$ and define $a +_7 b$ to be the remainder when $a + b$ is divided by 7. So, for example, $5 + 6 = 4 \bmod 7$. Show that $(Z_7, +_7)$ is a group. (To prove associativity without considering all the cases requires more theory than we are developing here. So just illustrate associativity with a few examples.)

Exercise 5: Let $Z_9 = \{0, 1, 2, 3, 4, 5, 6, 7, 8\}$ and define multiplication mod 9 in a manner analogous to multiplication mod 7. Show that $(Z_9, \cdot_9)$ is *not* a group. What elements would you have to evict from Z_9 so that the remaining set was a group under mod 9 multiplication? Justify your answer by showing that your new system satisfies the group properties. (To prove associativity without considering all the cases requires more theory than we are developing here. So just illustrate associativity with a few examples.)

And now we come to our last example of a finite group.

Project 3

Do the following exercises. Let $R = \{1, 2, 3\}$ and let $P(R)$ be *the power set of R,* that is, the set of all subsets of R. So, for example, one element of $P(R)$ is $\{1, 3\}$.

Exercise 1: List the eight elements of $P(R)$.

We define the operation Δ on $P(R)$ as follows: If A and B are elements of $P(R)$, then $A \Delta B = (A \cup B) - (A \cap B)$. So, for example, $\{1, 3\} \Delta \{2, 3\} = \{1, 2, 3\} - \{3\} = \{1, 2\}$.

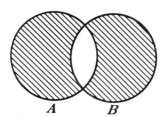

The shaded portion corresponds to $A \Delta B$.

We read $A \Delta B$ as "the symmetric difference of A and B."

Exercise 2: Make a chart that contains the symmetric difference of each two elements of $P(R)$.

Exercise 3: Illustrate that Δ is an associate operation on $P(R)$. You may do so either by drawing an appropriate picture or by considering some instances of associativity.

Exercise 4: What is the Δ identity in $P(R)$? Find the Δ inverse of each element of $P(R)$.

Further Investigations

Analyze the permutations of the vertices of a square or a pentagon or some other regular two- or three-dimensional figure. Look more closely at several different modular systems. There are many fascinating relationships to uncover.

If you would like to learn more about the general theory of groups, look in a college library for any textbook about modern algebra or abstract algebra. Such books will contain chapters on groups and other algebraic structures.

Teacher Notes

The student reading this chapter should be familiar with the following notions:
- commutative and associative properties
- functions and mapping
- equilateral triangles, altitudes
- clock arithmetic
- set notation, union, intersection, and difference of sets
- operation

Project 1

Exercises 1 and 2 have no written answers.

Exercise 3: g maps 1 to 3, 2 to 1, and 3 to 2.

Exercise 4: i corresponds to flipping the triangle over the altitude from the vertex numbered 2. j corresponds to flipping the triangle over the altitude from the vertex numbered 3.

Exercise 5:

*	e	f	g	h	i	j
e	e	f	g	h	i	j
f	f	g	e	i	j	h
g	g	e	f	j	h	i
h	h	j	i	e	g	f
i	i	h	j	f	e	g
j	j	i	h	g	f	e

Exercise 6:

Function	e	f	g	h	i	j
*Inverse of function	e	g	f	h	i	j

Exercise 7: The student should cite at least two instances of associativity. Regarding the note: There are $6 \times 6 \times 6 = 216$ instances of associativity, but only $5 \times 5 \times 5 = 125$ do not involve the function e. Of these 125, five involve using the same function three times. So there are several different possible "correct answers" to this question.

If $l, m,$ and n are all permutations of a set S and x is an element of S, then $((l \circ m) \circ n)(x) = (l \circ m)(n(x)) = l(m(n(x))) = l((m \circ n)(x)) = (l \circ (m \circ n))(x)$

Exercise 8: $j * i = f$

Exercise 9: a) e   b) f

Exercise 10: a) f   b) h

Exercise 11: Function composition is not commutative, so the error is in going from $x * j = f$ to $x * j * j = j * f$ (instead of $f * j$).

    a) If e and e' are both indentities of $(S, \circ)$, then
$$e' = e \circ e' = e.$$
    b) If b and c are both the inverse of a, then
$$c \circ (a \circ b) = c \circ e = c.$$
    But also
$$c \circ (a \circ b) = (c \circ a) \circ b = e \circ b = b.$$
    So
$$c = b.$$

Project 2

Exercise 1:

· 7	0	1	2	3	4	5	6
0	0	0	0	0	0	0	0
1	0	1	2	3	4	5	6
2	0	2	4	6	1	3	5
3	0	3	6	2	5	1	4
4	0	4	1	5	2	6	3
5	0	5	3	1	6	4	2
6	0	6	5	4	3	2	1

Exercise 2:

Element	1	2	3	4	5	6
Multiplicative inverse	1	4	5	2	3	6

Exercise 3: a) 2   *b)* 6

Exercise 4: 0 is the additive identity.

Element	0	1	2	3	4	5	6
Additive inverse	0	6	5	4	3	2	1

Exercise 5: 0, 3, and 6 have no multiplicative inverses. However, if we let $Z'_9 = \{1, 2, 4, 5, 7, 8\}$, then $Z'_9, \cdot_9)$ is a group.

Element	1	2	4	5	7	8
Multiplicative inverse	1	5	7	2	4	8

Project 3

Exercise 1: ϕ, {1}, {2}, {3}, {1,2}, {1,3}, {2,3}, {1,2,3}

Exercise 2:

Δ	ϕ	1	2	3	1,2	1,3	2,3	1,2,3
ϕ	ϕ	ϕ	ϕ	ϕ	ϕ	ϕ	ϕ	ϕ
1	ϕ	ϕ	1,2	1,3	2	3	1,2,3	2,3
2	ϕ	1,2	ϕ	2,3	1	1,2,3	3	1,3
3	ϕ	1,3	2,3	ϕ	1,2,3	1	2	1,2
1,2	ϕ	2	1	1,2,3	ϕ	2,3	1,3	3
1,3	ϕ	3	1,2,3	1	2,3	ϕ	1,2	2
2,3	ϕ	1,2,3	3	2	1,3	1,2	ϕ	1
1,2,3	ϕ	2,3	1,3	1,2	3	2	1	ϕ

Exercise 3:

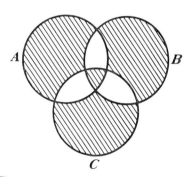

The shaded area corresponds to
$A \Delta (B \Delta C) = A \Delta (B \Delta C)$.

Exercise 4: ϕ is the identity. Each element of $P(R)$ is its own inverse, since $(A \cup A) - (A \cap A) = A - A = \phi$.

Transfinite Numbers

ROBERT L. MOORE

> The infinite! No other question has ever moved so
> profoundly the spirit of man.
>
> David Hilbert

HILBERT'S remark is correct: The notion of infinity evokes philosophical and theological stirrings as no other scientific concept can. Most people think of infinity as something absolute, unchangeable, and completely past human comprehension. In fact, none of these notions is quite correct. Mathematicians have been studying infinity for over fifty years and have discovered some surprising things, including the fact that there are different "sizes" of infinite sets, and that there is even an arithmetic of infinite numbers. This does not mean that the infinite has been completely tamed; many puzzles remain, some of which have forced a reexamination of the roots of mathematics and of logic itself. This guide will help you to understand some of the progress that has been made and some of the difficulties that have arisen.

Projects

Project 1

The essential building block in the theory of infinite (or "transfinite") numbers is the notion of a one-to-one correspondence between sets. The existence of a one-to-one correspondence can often be very surprising, particularly if one set "looks" much larger. To get some understanding of this basic concept, first read References 8 and 4 and the chapter on infinity in Reference 3.

Next, do *one* of the following exercises.

1. Let B be the set of points on a line (not a segment) and let A be the set of points on a segment of B with finite length. (For instance, B might be the x-axis and A the interval between -1 and 1, that is, A consists of all numbers x so that $-1 < x < 1$.) Find a one-to-one correspondence between the sets A and B. Write out your correspondence function, either in words or as an equation, in such a way that each point x in A completely determines a corresponding point y in B.

2. Let A be the set of points in the interior of a line segment of length one and let B be the set of points inside a square of side one. Find a one-to-one correspondence between A and B.

3. Let A be the set of positive integers and let B be the set of positive rational numbers; that is, fractions of the form p/q where p and q are integers. Find a one-to-one correspondence between the sets A and B.

Guide: First, try to do the exercises without help. If you get stuck, you can find help for exercises 2 and 3 in chapter 11 of Reference 2. In exercise 1, first find a correspondence between B and the interval between $-\pi$ and π (i.e., $-\pi < x < \pi$) by examining some trigonometric functions. Then modify this function so that the correspondence is between A and B.

Project 2

Georg Cantor was the founder of the theory of transfinite numbers. One of his most important legacies is the *Cantor diagonal process,* which is the basis for many proofs involving infinite sets. In Reference 8, the diagonal process is used to prove that there is no one-to-one correspondence between the set **N** of natural numbers and the set P (**N**) of subsets of **N**. Follow this example to prove *one* of the following facts. Write out your proof carefully.

1. Let C be any infinite set. Then there is no one-to-one correspondence between C and $P(C)$ (the symbol P is defined in Reference 8.

2. There is no one-to-one correspondence between **N** and the set (0,1) of real numbers x such that $0 < x < 1$.

Guide: If you get stuck on exercise 2, check Reference 3. Here is how to start on exercise 1. Let the elements of C be represented by the letter c (just as n represented an element of **N**). Suppose that each c corresponds (in some way) to a subset K_c of C. Now show that there is a subset K of C that is not one of the sets K_c.

One of the most important conjectures in the history of mathematics was the *continuum hypothesis* (see Reference 8). If you want to pursue the study of different sizes of transfinite numbers, read about the continuum hypothesis in Reference 5.

Project 3

Mathematics is more than just equations and proofs—it is also inspiration and toil, joy and frustration, clear deduction, and (sometimes) blind luck. Reading biographies of mathematicians seldom helps us understand their work, but it can help us to put that work into historical perspective and to appreciate the fact that geniuses are also human beings. Read the article on Cantor in Reference 1. Write the answer to the following questions.

- When did Cantor live? What nationality was he?
- Did his first paper mark him as a genius?
- What studies led him to attack the problem of "actual infinities"?
- Which mathematician led the opposition to his "actual infinities"?
- What factor in Cantor's earlier years contributed to his occasional breakdowns?
- Which mathematicians found paradoxes that threatened the theory of transfinite numbers? What does the term *antinomy* mean?

Project 4

The work of Cantor and the difficulties unearthed by Russell and others contributed to a reexamination of the nature of mathematics and its relationship to reality. Three schools of thought emerged in the early part of the twentieth century: logicism, intuitionism, and formalism. Write an essay of 500 to 1000 words in which you describe these points of view; you should mention some of the proponents of these views. Which view do you think is correct? Why?

Guide: Chapters 41 and 51 of Reference 6, Reference 7, and the article by Hahn in Reference 4 will help you complete this requirement.

Further Investigations

Another fascinating related subject is the study of ordinal numbers, which deal with the ordering of sets. You can find out about orderings and ordinal numbers as well as many other subjects in Reference 5.

REFERENCES

1. Bell, Eric Temple. *Men of Mathematics*. New York: Simon & Schuster, 1962.
2. Dantzig, Tobias. *Number—the Language of Science*. New York: Macmillan, 1954.
3. Gamow, George. *One, Two, Three, Infinity*. New York: Viking Press, 1947.
4. Hahn, Hans. "Infinity." In *The World of Mathematics*, edited by James R. Newman. New York: Simon & Schuster, 1956.
5. Halmos, P. R. *Naive Set Theory*. New York: Van Nostrand, 1960.
6. Kline, Morris. *Mathematical Thought from Ancient to Modern Times*. New York: Oxford University Press, 1972.
7. Meschkowski, Herbert. *Evolution of Mathematical Thought*. San Francisco: Holden-Day, 1965.
8. Moore, Robert L. "How to Count to Infinity." *Alabama Journal of Mathematics* 5 (Spring 1981): 22–26. (Reprints available from the author at Department of Mathematics, University of Alabama, University, AL 35486.)

Teacher Notes

Project 1

1. One possibility for a correspondence function between the intervals $(-1,1)$ and $(-\infty,\infty)$ is $f(x) = \tan(\pi x)$. There are other possible answers, but any acceptable function must be one-to-one (i.e., no values of $f(x)$ should be repeated for different x's) and onto (i.e., every real number in $(-\infty,\infty)$ must be $f(x)$ for some x). This last remark pertains to exercises 1, 2, and 3.

2. Let the points on the line be represented by decimals: $0.x_1x_2x_3\ldots$, where x_1, x_2, and so on, represent the digits. Represent points in the square by pairs of decimals: $(0.x_1x_2x_3\ldots, 0.y_1y_2y_3\ldots)$. A possible correspondence is to let each point in the square correspond to the point on the line constructed this way: $0.x_1y_1x_2y_2x_3y_3\ldots$. Actually the function so constructed is not quite onto (e.g., the number $0.1000\ldots$ isn't associated with any point *inside* the square), but the main idea is contained in it, and it would be an acceptable answer. To modify this function to make it onto is merely a technical matter; if the student can do this, so much the better.

3. Rational numbers have the form p/q, where p and q are integers. Order the positive rationals according to the sum of numerator and denominator: first, those whose sum is 1, then 2, and so on.

$$\frac{0}{1}, \frac{0}{2}, \frac{1}{1}, \frac{0}{3}, \frac{1}{2}, \frac{2}{1}, \frac{0}{4}, \frac{1}{3}, \frac{2}{2}, \frac{3}{1}, \ \ldots$$

Next strike out any numbers equal to earlier ones.

$$\frac{0}{1}, \cancel{\frac{0}{2}}, \frac{1}{1}, \cancel{\frac{0}{3}}, \frac{1}{2}, \frac{2}{1}, \cancel{\frac{0}{4}}, \frac{1}{3}, \cancel{\frac{2}{2}}, \frac{3}{1}, \ \ldots$$

Now associate integers with the remaining terms.

$$1 \longleftrightarrow \frac{0}{1} \qquad\qquad 4 \longleftrightarrow \frac{2}{1}$$

$$2 \longleftrightarrow \frac{1}{1} \qquad\qquad 5 \longleftrightarrow \frac{1}{3}$$

$$3 \longleftrightarrow \frac{1}{2} \qquad\qquad 6 \longleftrightarrow \frac{3}{1}$$
$$\vdots$$

It is difficult to write down this function algebraically, but it is clear that if any integer (say, 300) is given, the corresponding rational number can be worked out. This fact is enough to tell us that the function is well defined. As usual, other one-to-one and onto functions exist.

Project 2

1. The symbol P means "all the subsets of"; so $P(C)$ refers to the set of all subsets of the set C. The student is asked to prove that no one-to-one correspondence exists between C and $P(C)$. The student's proof, at a minimum, should contain something like this:

Suppose that some function is proposed that associates a subset of C with each point of C; say, K_c corresponds to c. We must show that there is a subset of C that corresponds to no point of C. Let S consist of all points c in C that are not members of their corresponding sets, that is, $S = \{c \ \varepsilon \ C : c \notin K_c\}$. Suppose there is a c such that $S = K_c$. If c is in S, then c is in K_c, but then, by definition of S, c is not in S. On the other hand, if c is not in S, then it cannot be true that $c \notin K_c$—that is, c is in K_c and hence in S. Thus, c is neither in S nor not in S, and it follows that our assumption that $S = K_c$ was false. Hence the collection $\{K_c\}$ does not exhaust $P(C)$.

Of course, the student may employ different notation—a rose by any other name, and so on. What appears above is the skeleton of a proof—some additional explanatory matter would be acceptable, though not required.

2. Here the student is asked to show that there is no one-to-one correspondence between the positive integers and the interval (0,1) of real numbers. Here is a sketch:

Any real number in (0,1) can be written as a decimal: $0.x_1 x_2 x_3. . .$, with digits $x_1, x_2, x_3, ...$ Suppose that some rule has been defined that associates one of these decimals to each natural number:

$$1 \longleftrightarrow 0.x_1 x_2 x_3 . . . \qquad\qquad 3 \longleftrightarrow 0.z_1 z_2 z_3 . . .$$
$$2 \longleftrightarrow 0.y_1 y_2 y_3 . . . \qquad\qquad \vdots$$

We construct a real number between 0 and 1 that does not appear in the right-hand column. First, choose a digit that differs from x_1, 0, and 9; call it a_1. Next, choose a digit that differs from y_2, 0, and 9; call it a_2. Next, choose a_3 that differs from z_3, 0, and 9. Proceed in this way, choosing for a_n a digit that differs from 0, 9, and the nth digit in the real number assigned to the integer n on the list.

Let $r = 0.a_1 a_2 a_3 . . . .$ The number r cannot be any of the real numbers already listed because it differs from the nth one in the nth place.

The fact that a_n differs from 0 and 9 is to ensure that we don't construct, for example, a number r of the form $0.1270000 . . .$, since in this case the number $0.126999 . . .$ might appear elsewhere on the list, and these numbers are equal.

Again, what appears here is only a skeleton—some connective tissue might be advisable.

Project 3

Short answers to the questions mentioned in this project follow. The student should, of course, know more than this.

- Cantor lived from 1845 to 1918. His mother was Jewish and his father was Danish; he was born in Russia and spent part of his childhood in Germany.

- Cantor's first paper concerned number theory and was a solid piece of work but did not establish him as a genius.

- Bell suggests that Cantor's study of Fourier series may have led to work on infinities.

- Kronecker (1823–1891) was Cantor's most outspoken opponent.

- Cantor's father insisted for some years that he pursue the study of engineering. His father finally relented, but damage was done to Cantor's self-esteem.

- Burali-Forti (1897) and Russell (1908) were among the mathematicians who discovered paradoxes in the very foundations of set theory.

Project 4

Three schools of mathematical philosophy can be briefly distinguished as follows:

- *Logicism,* founded by Russell and Whitehead, holds that mathematics is purely derivable from logic. The logicists attempted to shore up classical logic and mathematics in such a way that the controversial axiom of choice and the equally controversial concept of transfinite numbers could be accommodated.

- *Intuitionism,* founded by Kronecker and carried on by Brouwer, rejected most ideas of infinity. Their point of view was that the only solid portions of mathematics were those that could be based on the only mathematical concepts for which people have a "pure intuition"—namely, the natural numbers. The intuitionists rejected proofs of existence that did not construct the objects whose existence was asserted.

- *Formalism,* founded by Hilbert, agreed with logicism in developing mathematics and logic together. However, the formalists, unlike the logicists, wanted to divorce logic and mathematics from any "idealized" physical objects. In this view, all meaning is eliminated from the symbols, and mathematics becomes a completely semantic doctrine.

Pythagoras and His Theorem

GLORIA D. DONALDSON

THE Greek mathematician Pythagoras was born in the fifth century B.C. He founded the Pythagorean school of mathematics in Crotona, a Greek seaport in southern Italy. Pythagoras is credited with many contributions to the field of mathematics, some of which may actually have been made by his loyal students.

Projects

Project 1

Write a paper of at least 750 words about Pythagoras and the Pythagoreans.

Guide: References 1, 2, 3, 5, 6, 7, 8, 9, and 10 should be helpful. You may also find some useful information in an encyclopedia. Be sure to include what is known about the life of Pythagoras as well as the contributions the Pythagoreans made to mathematics.

Project 2

The Pythagorean theorem states that the square of the hypotenuse of a right triangle is equal to the sum of the squares of the other two sides. Demonstrate at least ten different proofs of this theorem, including those of Euclid, Leonardo da Vinci, and President James A. Garfield. Be able to explain any one of them on request.

Guide: There have been hundreds of proofs or demonstrations of the Pythagorean theorem. References 3, 4, 5, 6, 7, 9, and 10 as well as geometry textbooks are useful.

Project 3

1. Write a computer program that will generate Pythagorean triples from one number.
2. Write a computer program that will generate Pythagorean triples from two numbers.
3. A primitive Pythagorean triple is one in which the three natural numbers are relatively prime. Use your programs to find all the primitive triples of which the largest member of the triple is less than 100. How many are there?

Guide: There are two formulas that will be helpful in writing your programs. References 3, 5, 7, and 10 are useful, as are books on computer programming in BASIC. There are also sections on programming in most algebra textbooks.

Project 4

This project has three parts.

1. *Construct* a right triangle with a semicircle mounted on each side. Each side is the diameter of its semicircle. Prove that the sum of the areas of the semicircles on the legs is equal to the area of the semicircle on the hypotenuse.

2. *Construct* a right triangle with an equilateral triangle constructed on each side so that each side of the right triangle is a side of an equilateral triangle. Prove that the sum of the areas of the equilateral triangles on the legs equals the area of the equilateral triangle on the hypotenuse.

3. In like manner, *construct* a right triangle with a regular hexagon mounted on each side. Prove that the sum of the areas of the hexagons on the legs equals the area of the hexagon on the hypotenuse.

Guide: For exercise 1, you need to know how to find the area of a circle. For exercises 2 and 3, you need to know how to find the area of an equilateral triangle in terms of one of the sides.

Further Investigations

Pierre de Fermat (1601?–1665) was familiar with Pythagorean triples. He became curious about whether integral triples (x,y,z) exist such that $x^3 + y^3 = z^3$, $x^4 + y^4 = z^4$, and so on. Fermat's "last theorem" states that positive integers x, y, z, and n such that $x^n + y^n = z^n$ do not exist when $n > 2$. Even though Fermat claimed to have found a proof, there is no evidence to substantiate his claim. You may wish to investigate Fermat and his theorem.

Guide: References 1, 2, 3, 8, 9, and 10 are useful.

REFERENCES

1. Bell, Eric Temple. *Men of Mathematics.* 3d ed. New York: Simon & Schuster, 1965.
2. Bell, Eric Temple. *The Development of Mathematics.* 2d ed. New York: McGraw-Hill, 1945.
3. Eves, Howard. *An Introduction to the History of Mathematics.* 4th ed. New York: Holt, Rinehart & Winston, 1976.
4. Jacobs, Harold R. *Geometry.* San Francisco: W. H. Freeman & Co., 1974.
5. Kline, Morris. *Mathematical Thought from Ancient to Modern Times.* New York: Oxford University Press, 1956.
6. Linn, Charles F., ed. *The Ages of Mathematics.* 2 vols. Garden City, N.Y.: Doubleday & Co., 1977.
7. Loomis, Elisha S. *The Pythagorean Proposition.* Washington, D.C.: NCTM, 1968.
8. Newman, James R. *Men and Numbers.* New York: Simon & Schuster, 1956.
9. Newman, James R. *The World of Mathematics.* 4 vols. New York: Simon & Schuster, 1956.
10. National Council of Teachers of Mathematics. *Historical Topics for the Mathematics Classroom.* Thirty-first Yearbook. Washington, D.C.: The Council, 1969.

These are only some of the sources of information available. You may use any other sources that you find in the library. Your teacher may have some sources and may be able to suggest others.

Teacher Notes

Project 3

1 and 2. Encourage students to create their own programs. The following program is one that includes both parts of this project.

```
10    REM PROGRAM NAME:  TRIPLE
20    PRINT 'PYTHAGOREAN TRIPLE GENERATOR'
30    PRINT
40    PRINT 'DO YOU WISH TO USE ONE OR TWO NUMBERS'
50    PRINT 'TO GENERATE THE PYTHAGOREAN TRIPLES';
60    INPUT A$
70    PRINT
80    IF A$='TWO' GOTO 170
90    PRINT 'ENTER THE GENERATOR NUMBER';
100   INPUT M
110   LET M1=2*M
120   LET M2=M^2-1
130   LET M3=M^2+1
140   PRINT
150   PRINT 'THE TRIPLE GENERATED BY';M; 'IS' ;M1; ',' ;M2; ',' ;M3
160   GOTO 260
170   PRINT 'ENTER THE TWO GENERATOR'
180   PRINT 'NUMBERS SEPARATED BY A COMMA';
190   INPUT M,N
200   LET M1=2*M*N
210   LET M2=M^2-N^2
220   LET M3=M^2+N^2
230   IF M2<0 THEN LET M2=-M2
240   PRINT
250   PRINT 'THE TRIPLE GENERATED BY' ;M; 'AND' ;N; 'IS' ;M1; ',' ;M2; ',' ;M3
260   PRINT
270   PRINT 'DO YOU WISH TO CONTINUE'
280   INPUT A$
290   IF A$='YES' GOTO 30
300   PRINT
310   PRINT 'THANK YOU FOR ALLOWING ME TO GENERATE THESE'
320   PRINT 'INTERESTING PYTHAGOREAN TRIPLES. ISN'T THIS FUN?'
330   END
```

3. Solutions

1.	3	4	5	9.	16	63	65
2.	5	12	13	10.	20	21	29
3.	7	24	25	11.	28	45	53
4.	8	15	17	12.	33	56	65
5.	9	40	41	13.	36	77	85
6.	11	60	61	14.	39	80	89
7.	12	35	37	15.	48	55	73
8.	13	84	85	16.	65	72	97

Project 4

The students should have a good understanding of geometric constructions and proofs. You may need to tell them that a regular hexagon is composed of six equilateral triangles.

Topology

KATHERINE PEDERSEN

WELCOME to the world of topology! Welcome to a world where triangles and circles are equivalent, where you cannot tell the difference between a doughnut and a coffee cup, and where surfaces can have only one side!

This unit is designed to introduce you to the field of mathematics known as topology. The projects begin with a general overview of topology, focus on some early topological problems, and then develop the concepts of topologically equivalent spaces and topological properties. Suggestions for further study are made at the end.

Have fun! Enjoy your journey! Bon voyage!

Projects

Project 1

The purpose of this project is to introduce you to some of the mathematical concepts and to some of the mathematicians associated with the field of topology. You are not expected to understand the concepts at this time but only to recognize them as part of topology. The projects in this unit are organized so that you will ultimately understand the concepts.

1. Look up the word *topology* in several large encyclopedias or reference books. Write a paper of approximately 500 words (or three written pages) on topology.

2. Some of the words or phrases that you may find associated with topology follow.

One-to-one correspondence	Hausdorff
Continuous transformation	Möbius strip
Topological transformation	Sphere
Homeomorphism	Torus
Topological property	Klein bottle
Metric	Four-color problem

Include and discuss briefly at least four of these words or phrases in your paper.

3. Many mathematicians are associated with topology. The following are some of the names you might find in your reading: Leonhard Euler, Karl Friedrich Gauss, August F. Möbius, Georg Cantor, Henri Poincaré, G. F. B. Riemann, L. E. J. Brouwer, and Solomon Lefshetz. Include biographical data in your paper and discuss the contributions of at least three of these mathematicians to the field of topology.

Guide: Most major encyclopedias contain a reference on topology. Reference 8 and Reference 9 contain articles that emphasize mathematical concepts. Relevant material might also be found in References 7, 16, and 21. Historical data can be found in References 4, 11, 17, and 19.

Project 2

Project 2 might be subtitled "A Look into the Folklore of Topology." The field of topology did not come into being at a specific time, date, and place. Rather, it evolved as similar mathematical concepts were used by mathematicians to solve apparently dissimilar problems.

One of the problems of interest to early topologists involved the concept of the "sidedness" of a geometric surface. A surface is said to be *one-sided* if, for any two points on the surface, it is possible to construct a path on the surface from one point to the other such that the path does not cross an edge of the surface. The Möbius strip, named after the German mathematician August F. Möbius, is an example of a one-sided surface. A cylindrical tube, open on both ends, is not a one-sided surface, since any path from a point on the inside of the cylinder to a point on the outside of the cylinder *must* cross an edge.

The Möbius strip played a part in the formation of another topological concept. A simple closed curve is said to *separate a surface* if the simple closed curve lies on the surface and if cutting along the simple closed curve results in separating the surface into two pieces. A moment's thought should convince you that any simple closed curve drawn on the surface of a sphere will separate the sphere. It is not so obvious that there is a simple closed curve that can be drawn in the Möbius strip and that does *not* separate the strip.

The four-color problem is a problem in topology that was formulated over a hundred years ago and not solved until 1976. The four-color problem asks, What is the least number of colors needed to color a planar map so that regions with a common border are never given the same color? (Areas meeting in the manner of the states of Utah and New Mexico or Arizona and Colorado are not considered to have a common boundary.) Since the later years of the nineteenth century, it has been known that five colors are always sufficient. It is not difficult to find maps of areas that require four colors—New York, Connecticut, Massachusetts, and the Atlantic Ocean, for example. The question remained: Are four colors *always* sufficient? Since July 1976, the answer has been yes. The problem was solved by Kenneth Appel, Wolfgang Haken, and John Koch. (The first two authors are from the University of Illinois and the third is from Wilkes College.) The solution was published under the title "Every Planar Map Is Four Colorable" in the September 1977 issue of the *Illinois Journal of Mathematics*. It is always significant when a mathematics problem of such long standing is solved. The solution to the four-color problem is unique in that it was accomplished through the use of computers.

To satisfy Project 2, do *one* of the following two activities.

1. Prepare a presentation covering the topics of the "sidedness" of surfaces and of simple closed curves that separate surfaces. Include in your presentation the following:

a) Explain how to construct a Möbius strip and do so.

b) Demonstrate that the Möbius strip is one sided.

c) Discuss whether or not the following surfaces are one sided: a cylinder, a disk, and a "Möbius strip" with a double twist.

d) Demonstrate that any simple closed curve on a sphere separates the sphere.

e) Give an example of a simple closed curve on the Möbius strip that does not separate the strip.

2. Prepare a presentation on the four-color problem. Include the following exercises in your presentation:

a) State the four-color problem and give the history of it.

b) Give examples of planar maps (i.e., maps drawn on a flat surface) that require two colors, three colors, and four colors.

c) Show an example of a map drawn on the surface of the torus (i.e., a hollow inner tube) that requires five colors.

Guide: You are strongly encouraged to use experimentation to satisfy Project 2. Books that may be of interest are References 5 and 12. An explanation of how to construct a Möbius strip is found in References 1, 6, 8, and 10. Several pairs of points should be chosen to illustrate the one sidedness of the Möbius strip. The choice of points should include a point p and the point p', which appears to be directly under p on the "other side" of the Möbius strip. A decision on the one sidedness of the other surfaces should be made only after several pairs of points are chosen on each surface discussed.

The discussion of simple closed curves separating or not separating a surface should include examples of various simple closed curves on the surfaces. You are encouraged to generalize from your examples.

The short story called "The No-Sided Professor," by Martin Gardner (Reference 14), provides a humorous approach to the concept of sidedness. You will certainly want to read it if a copy is available.

Information on the four-color problem is available in References 6, 8, and 10. A search of news magazines published around September 1977 may provide interesting insights into the public's reaction (or lack of it!) to the solution of a century-old mathematics problem. Once you understand the statement of the four-color problem, experiment to find the examples called for in the presentation. Another Martin Gardner short story, "The Island of Five Colors" (Reference 13), is a light-hearted approach to one person's attempt to solve the four-color problem. Read this story if a copy is available. In light of the solution to the four-color problem by Appel, Haken, and Koch, do you think Martin Gardner would write the same story today?

Project 3

Topology is defined, in a rather circular fashion, as the study of topological properties. Topological properties are properties preserved under topological transformations. Topological transformations are called *homeomorphisms.* A homeomorphism is a continuous one-to-one correspondence from one set of points to another set of points such that the inverse transformation is also a continuous one-to-one correspondence.

You know intuitively that the requirement of one-to-one correspondence restricts a homeomorphism from overlapping a figure onto itself. The correspondence between the line segment and the circle depicted in figure 1 is not a homeomorphism because the two endpoints of the segment overlap to form the circle.

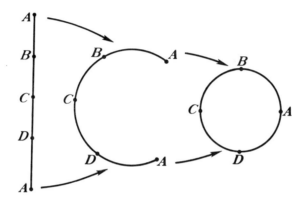

Fig. 1

In contrast, consider the correspondence depicted in figure 2, where each point *x* of the square corresponds to the point *x'* of the circle such that *O, x,* and *x'* are collinear and appear in that order. This correspondence defines a one-to-one correspondence between the square and the circle.

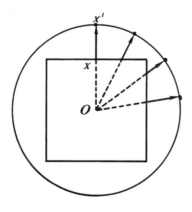

Fig. 2

The requirement that a homeomorphism and its inverse be continuous translates into everyday language to mean that the homeomorphism cannot "tear" the figure. For example, a torus (a hollow inner tube) and a cylinder are not homeomorphic because the torus would have to be "torn" or "cut" to make it into a cylinder. (See fig. 3.)

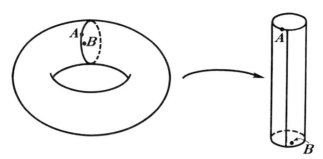

Fig. 3

Another intuitive translation of continuity is to say that points close to each other are associated with points close to each other. In figure 3, *A* is on the circle and *B* is slightly off the circle. If the circle *A* corresponds to the top edge of the cylinder, then *B* can be thought of as corresponding to a point very close to the bottom edge of the cylinder. Thus, the correspondence is *not* continuous, since *B* is close to *A* but the point associated with *B* is not close to the point associated with *A*.

Notice that in figure 2, points close to *x* are associated with points close to *x'* and vice versa. The correspondence depicted in figure 2 is continuous. Thus, the correspondence is a homeomorphism.

Project 3

Complete exercises 1, 2, and *either* 3 or 4.

1. Show that a triangle, a square, and, in fact, any polygon is homeomorphic to a circle.

2. The function $f(x) = \tan x$ is a homeomorphism if the domain of the function is the open interval $(-\pi/2, \pi/2)$. What two sets of points does this homeomorphism show to be topologically equivalent?

3. A remark often heard in the company of topologists is that a topologist "cannot tell the difference between a coffee cup and a doughnut." Using pliable material such as clay, illustrate how a doughnut can be transformed into a coffee cup without overlapping the points of the doughnut and without tearing it.

4. The term *stereographic projection* is used to refer to a particular correspondence between the points that make up a sphere minus the north pole and the points that make up an infinite plane. Describe a stereographic projection and justify why it is a homeomorphism.

Guide: Project 4 involves researching stereographic projection. Suggested references are large encyclopedias, geometry books, and geography books. Projects 1, 2, and 3 are best approached through experimentation. References 5, 12, 15, and 18 may be useful.

Project 4

Topological properties are properties preserved under homeomorphisms. The concept of preserving properties under certain correspondences is not new to you. In geometry, a congruence between two triangles is a correspondence between the set of points composing one triangle and the set of points composing the other triangle. A congruence is defined such that a segment is mapped to a segment of the same length. Also, an angle is associated with an angle of the same measure. Thus, we say that length and angle measure are preserved under a congruence.

Complete exercises 1, 2, and 3.

1. Show that angle measure is not a topological property by constructing a homeomorphism between a square and a triangle.

2. Show that length is not a topological property by considering the homeomorphism $f(x) = \tan x$ with domain the open interval $(-\pi/2, \pi/2)$.

3. You may be wondering if there are, in fact, any topological properties. There are! Some of these properties are connected, compact, Hausdorff, Euler characteristic, and winding number. Choose one of these properties or choose another topological property you may have encountered in your readings. Write a short paper discussing the property you choose. Include in your paper a definition of the property, examples of sets of points that possess the property, and examples of sets of points that do not possess the property.

Guide: Exercises 1 and 2 of Project 4 are related to exercises 1 and 2 of Project 3, respectively. Several encyclopedias, in particular References 8 and 9, discuss topological properties. You may also find References 5, 12, 15, and 18 of value.

Further Investigations

The projects in this unit allow choices. You might enjoy completing all the projects listed. If you are interested in pursuing the study of topology, you might investigate the concept of a *metric space.* References 5, 12, 15, and 18 would be appropriate.

REFERENCES

1. *Academic American Encyclopedia,* vol. 19. Danbury, Conn.: Grolier, 1983.
2. Appel, Kenneth, and Wolfgang Haken. "Every Planar Map Is Four Colorable: Part 1." *Illinois Journal of Mathematics* 21 (3) (1977):429–90.
3. Appel, Kenneth, Wolfgang Haken, and John Koch. "Every Planar Map Is Four Colorable: Part 2." *Illinois Journal of Mathematics* (3) (1977):491–567.
4. Boyer, Carl B. *A History of Mathematics.* New York: John Wiley & Sons, 1968.
5. Chinn, William G., and Norman E. Steinrod. *First Concepts of Topology.* New York: Random House, 1966.
6. *Collier's Encyclopedia,* vol. 22. New York: Macmillan Educational Corp., 1979.
7. Courant, Richard, and Herbert E. Robbins. *What Is Mathematics?,* chap. 5. London: Oxford University Press, 1941.
8. *Encyclopaedia Britannica,* vol. 22. Chicago: Encyclopaedia Britannica, 1970.
9. *Encyclopedia Americana, International Edition,* vol. 26. Danbury, Conn.: Americana Corp., 1979.
10. *Encyclopedia International,* vol. 18. Manila: Lexicon Publications, 1979.
11. Eves, Howard. *An Introduction to the History of Mathematics.* 4th ed. New York: Holt, Rinehart & Winston, 1976.
12. Flegg, Graham. *From Geometry to Topology.* London: The English Universities Press Ltd., 1974.
13. Gardner, Martin. "The Island of Five Colors." In *Fantasia Mathematica,* edited by Clifton Fadiman. New York: Simon & Schuster, 1958.
14. Gardner, Martin. "No-Sided Professor." In *Fantasia Mathematica,* edited by Clifton Fadiman. New York: Simon & Schuster, 1958.
15. Kahn, Donald. *Topology, an Introduction to the Point-Set and Algebraic Areas.* Baltimore: Williams & Wilkins, 1975.
16. Kasner, Edward, and James Newman. *Mathematics and the Imagination,* pp. 265–98. New York: Simon & Schuster, 1940.
17. Kramer, Edna. *The Nature and Growth of Modern Mathematics.* New York: Hawthorn Books, 1970.
18. Mendelson, Bert. *Introduction to Topology.* 3d ed. Boston: Allyn & Bacon, 1975.
19. National Council of Teachers of Mathematics. *Historical Topics for the Mathematics Classroom.* Thirty-first Yearbook. Washington, D.C.: The Council, 1969.
20. Rosskopf, Myron F., Joan L. Levine, and Bruce R. Vogeli. *Geometry, a Perspective View,* chaps. 14 and 15. New York: McGraw-Hill Book Co., 1969.
21. Tucker, Albert W., and Herbert S. Bailey, Jr. "Topology." *Scientific American,* January 1950, pp. 18–24.
22. *World Book Encyclopedia,* vol. 19. Chicago: Field Enterprises Educational Corp., 1974.

Teacher Notes

Project 2

1. *a*) To construct a Möbius strip, a rectangular strip of paper is given one twist before the ends are joined together. The construction of a Möbius band is depicted in figure 4. The source of figure 4 is Reference 6.

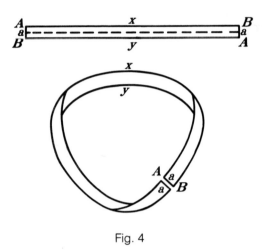

Fig. 4

b) Points *P* and *P'* as shown in figure 5 should be considered.

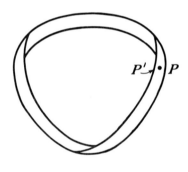

Fig. 5

c) The cylinder, disk, and "Möbius strip" with a *double* twist are two-sided.

d) The simple closed curve on the Möbius strip that corresponds to the line drawn horizontally through the middle of the rectangle in figure 4 produces a simple closed curve that does not separate the Möbius strip.

2. Figure 6 is one of the possible answers for exercise *b*, and figure 7 is one of the possible answers satisfying exercise *c*.

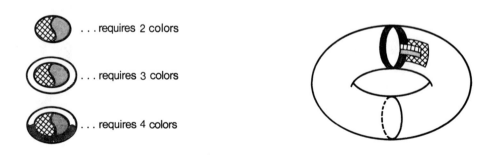

Fig. 6

Fig. 7

Project 3

1. The following correspondence (fig. 8) indicates that a triangle and a circle are homeomorphic. Many other choices for homeomorphisms are possible.

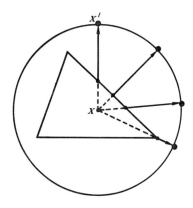

Fig. 8

2. The function $f(x) = \tan x$ with domain $(-\pi/2, \pi/2)$ is a homeomorphism between $(-\pi/2, \pi/2)$ and the set of real numbers. This shows that the open interval of $(-\pi/2, \pi/2)$ is homeomorphic to the entire real line.

3. The following illustration (fig. 9) of transforming a doughnut into a coffee cup is from Reference 12, page 58.

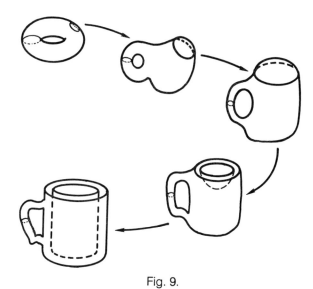

Fig. 9.

4. Let the sphere S be tangent to the plane E at A. Let O, the north pole, be diametrically opposite A on the sphere. Define a mapping from $S - \{O\}$ to E such that for $x \in S$, x is associated with $x' \in E$ such that O, x, and x' are collinear and x is between O and x'.

Geometric Inversion

KATHRYN M. BAALMAN

THE inversion of a plane in a circle seems originally to have been a generalization of ordinary reflection in a straight line. A simple example is given by the reflection of the plane in a given straight line as in a mirror. Inversions are sometimes called circular reflections because to a certain approximation they represent the relationship between an image and its original in reflection by a convex circular mirror.

Inversion is a transformation that associates with each point P of some geometric figure another point P'. In figure 1, point P' is said to be the *inverse* to point P with respect to the given circle. Point P' is the inverse to point P with respect to the given circle, called the *circle of inversion*, if and only if (1) points O, P, and P' all lie on the same ray, and (2) $OP * OP' = k^2$ (* means multiply) where O is the center of the circle and k is the radius.

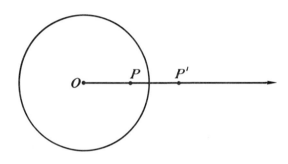

Fig. 1

Point O is the *center* (or the *pole*) of inversion, and k is the *radius* of inversion. The square of the radius is known as the *degree* (or *power*) of inversion. By letting the circle of inversion have a unit radius, $k = 1$, the distances of the inverse points from the center of inversion are reciprocal numbers, that is, $OP = 1/OP'$ and $OP' = 1/OP$.

The pole of inversion has no inverse but can be thought of as inverting into an infinite point. In working with a plane "punctured" at the pole, that is, a plane with O not considered, we may define an inversion as a 1-1 mapping of the plane, punctured at the pole of inversion, onto itself (see Further Investigations at the end of the projects).

Projects

Project 1

Given: k
O ⊢————————⊣ P

Point O is the center of inversion, k is the radius of inversion, and OP is the distance of the given point P from the center of inversion.

Using this given information, locate the image P' of the point P following the directions for each method of construction as given. Write a deductive proof for cases 1 and 2 of Method C that follows.

Method A: Fourth proportional. Draw the circle of inversion O, using the given radius k. Starting at point O, mark off the length OP on a ray. (P will be inside the circle.) On a separate drawing, use lengths OP and k and construct a fourth proportional to find the length of OP'. (Remember that $OP * OP' = k^2$.)

Using the length OP' that you find by this construction, locate the point P' on the ray OP. The point P' is the inverse of point P with respect to the circle of inversion O and radius of inversion k. Now repeat Method A with $k = 1/2\ k$. This will put the point P outside the circle of inversion. Use the same length OP. This time your inverse point, P', will lie inside the circle of inversion.

Method B: A tangent, secant theorem. Draw the circle of inversion O and ray OP as in Method A. On a separate drawing, find the length of OP' by using the following theorem: *If a tangent and a secant intersect outside a circle, the tangent is the mean proportional between the secant and its external segment.* Use this length OP' to locate point P', the inverse to point P, on ray OP. (*Hint:* Let $k =$ the tangent length, $OP =$ the external segment, $OP' =$ the entire secant.) Repeat Method B with a new length $k = 1/2\ k$, so as to put the point P outside the circle of inversion. Use the same length OP. Your inverse point should lie inside the circle of inversion.

Method C:

Case 1. Point P inside the circle of inversion. Draw the circle of inversion and ray OP as before. Construct through point P a perpendicular to the ray OP. Label the resulting chord TT_1, with points T and T_1 being the extremities of the chord. Construct tangents to the circle at points T and T_1. Point P', the intersection of these tangents, is the inverse of point P. Write a deductive proof to show that $OP * OP' = k^2$.

Case 2. Point P outside the circle of inversion. Draw the circle of inversion with radius k and center O. Using $OP = 2 * OP$, draw ray OP. With center at P and radius PO, intersect circle O at points A_1 and A_2. With radius A_1O and A_2O (centers at A_1 and A_2) draw circular arcs. P', the point of intersection of the two arcs, is the inverse of point P. Write a deductive proof to show that $OP * OP' = k^2$. (*Hint:* Draw line A_1A_2 and label the point where it intersects line OP as Q. Use the Pythagorean theorem on triangles A_1PQ and A_1OQ.)

Project 2

Given the circle of inversion and a circle through the center of inversion as shown in figure 2, find the inverse of each of seven points on the given circle to determine the locus of the inverse image. Use any of the methods you have learned. When you have found the seven inverse points, state a theorem about the locus of the inverse of a circle that passes through the center of inversion.

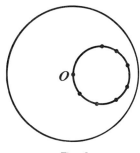

Fig. 2

Project 3

Study the following list of theorems on inverse curves. As you go through the theorems and their corollaries, keep in mind the basic ideas that follow from the definition:

- The inverse of a point inside the circle is a point outside the circle.
- The inverse of a point outside the circle is a point inside the circle.
- A point on the circle inverts into itself.
- The pole has no inverse but may be thought of as inverting into an infinite point.

List of theorems

1. The inverse of a straight line through the pole of inversion is the line itself.
2. The inverse of a line not through the pole is a circle passing through the pole of inversion.

COROLLARY

- *A line exterior to the circle of inversion gives a circle through the pole and interior to the circle of inversion.*
- *A line intersecting the circle of inversion inverts into a circle passing through the two points of intersection and also the pole of inversion.*

3. A circle through the center transforms into a line not through the center of inversion.
4. A circle not through the center of inversion inverts into another circle also not through the center.

COROLLARY

A circle concentric with the circle of inversion inverts into another circle also concentric with the circle of inversion.

Exercises. Using this list of theorems, the definition of inversion, and also what you discovered from your constructions in Project 1, make a sketch of the original figure and then sketch and describe the inverse of each of the following geometric figures.

Example: A line tangent to the circle of inversion

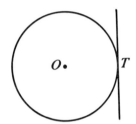

Sketch of original curve

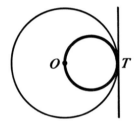

Sketch of inverse curve

Description of inverse curve

The inverse image of a line tangent to the circle of inversion is a circle tangent internally to the circle of inversion and passing through the pole. (*Note:* By corollary 1 of theorem 2, a line exterior to the circle of inversion gives a circle through the pole. Since any point on the circle is its own inverse, the image circle is also tangent internally to the circle of inversion, with the point *T* inverting into itself.)

1. The circle of inversion
2. *a)* A point *P* inside the circle of inversion
   b) A point *P* outside the circle of inversion
   c) The center of inversion
3. *a)* A line through the center of inversion
   b) A line not through the center of inversion and exterior to the circle of inversion
   c) A line not through the center of inversion but intersecting the circle of inversion
4. *a)* A circle not through the center of inversion and also inside the circle of inversion
   b) A circle not through the center of inversion and outside the circle of inversion
   c) A circle outside the circle of inversion and tangent to it
5. *a)* A circle through the center of inversion and also tangent to the circle of inversion
   b) A circle through the center of inversion and inside the circle of inversion
   c) A circle through the center of inversion and also intersecting the circle of inversion
6. A circle concentric with and inside the circle of inversion
7. A circle concentric with and outside the circle of inversion

Project 4

Properties that are not altered by geometric transformations are known as invariants. In the inversion transformation, angles are such an invariant. This property produces very useful consequences. In particular, tangent curves will be inverted into tangent curves. A special case of this invariant property is a circle that intersects the circle of inversion orthogonally (at right angles). Such a circle is transformed into itself.

Exercises. Keeping in mind this invariance of angles, sketch the original curve, then sketch and describe each of the following transformations. Remember, the pole of inversion has no inverse, hence circles "tangent" at the pole are "punctured" circles (i.e., are not sharing a common point).

1. Two parallel lines not through the pole, both lines outside and on the same side of the circle of inversion

2. A family of parallel lines on the same side of O

3. A circle through the pole and a line tangent to that circle. The given circle lies inside the circle of inversion.

4. A circle through the pole and a line tangent to that circle. The given circle is also tangent internally to the circle of inversion.

5. Two externally tangent circles, located inside the circle of inversion, with the point of "tangency" at the pole

6. Two externally tangent circles, neither of which passes through the pole but both being internal to the circle of inversion

7. Two externally tangent circles, neither of which passes through the pole of inversion and both circles lying outside the circle of inversion

Project 5

Several constructions in Euclidean geometry can be performed from the standpoint of geometric inversion and proved by using the definition of inversion. Follow the directions given to perform each of the following constructions.

1. *Bisecting a line segment.* Given the line segment AB, draw two circles having length AB as radius and centers at B and A. Extend AB through B to form the diameter AC for the circle that has its center at B. This will make $AB = BC$. The circle of inversion for the construction will have its pole at A and a radius equal to AB. Locate C', the inverse of C with respect to this inversion, and then using the definition of inversion, prove that C' is the desired midpoint of AB. (Prove that $2 * AC' = AB$.)

2. *Locating the center of a circle.* In the Euclidean construction, a convenient way to locate the center of a given circle is to construct the perpendicular bisector to two chords and determine their point of intersection. The center of a circle may also be located by using the concept of inversion.

Choosing any point P on the circumference of the given circle as the pole of inversion, draw a circle of inversion intersecting the given circle at points R and S. With these points as centers and radii RP and SP, the circles thus drawn will intersect at some point Q. The desired center of the circle will be the point Q', the inverse of point Q with respect to the circle of inversion. Complete the construction (by any method) to locate the point Q'.

Project 6

The Peaucellier inversor is a linkage used to convert circular motion into straight line motion. It is basically an inversor that is used to trace out a circle and its inverse. The linkage is made of a rhombus $ABCD$ pivoted at its vertices and a pair of equal rigid bars hinged at O and at B and D (see fig. 3).

The points O, A, C, and the midpoint E of BD all lie on the perpendicular bisector of DB. A and C are inverse points in the inversion that has as a circle of inversion a circle centered at O and a radius that is a leg of a right triangle with hypotenuse of length OD and leg AD.

If a rigid bar is attached to a fixed point M as shown in the drawing, with $MA = MO$, the point A will trace a circle passing through the center of inversion O as the point C describes a straight line perpendicular to MO, the line being the inverse to the circle.

1. Prove that A and C are inverse images with the circle of inversion and radius described above (i.e., prove that $OA * OC = OD^2 - AD^2$).

2. Make a Peaucellier inversor using bars made of cardboard or thin strips of wood, such as Popsicle sticks. Draw a circle of inversion O and a circle with center M passing through O. Using your inversor, trace the image of circle M. (Turn in your inversor along with your completed packet.)

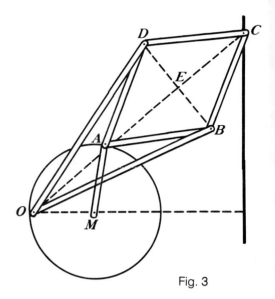

Fig. 3

Project 7

Some inversions form interesting patterns. Find the inverse curves of each of the following in a neat and accurate drawing.

1. A circumscribed equilateral triangle, circumscribed about the circle of inversion

2. A circumscribed pentagram (a five-pointed star formed by extending the sides of a regular pentagon), circumscribed about the circle of inversion

3. An inscribed pentagram, inscribed in the circle of inversion

Further Investigations

When the center of inversion is at the center of the checkerboard and a radius of inversion is equal to 1½ times the length of a single square, the entire checkerboard (representing the plane) will invert into itself. The inverted pattern lies partly inside and partly outside the circle, with the outer edges unbounded. Placing the center of inversion in the middle of a single square and using the radius given above, attempt to transform a part of the plane as described.

REFERENCES

1. Baravalle, Herman V. "Transformations of Curves by Inversion." *Scripta Mathematica* 14 (1948):113–25, 266–72.
2. Bell, Eric Temple. *Men of Mathematics.* New York: Simon & Schuster, 1937.
3. Bruyr, Donald L. *Geometrical Models and Demonstrations.* Portland, Maine: J. Weston Walch, 1963.
4. Casey, J. *A Sequel to the First Six Books of Euclid, Part I.* London, 1910.
5. Coolidge, J. L. *Treatise on the Circle and the Sphere.* Oxford, 1916.
6. Courant, Richard, and Herbert Robbins. *What Is Mathematics?* New York: Oxford University Press, 1961.
7. Court, Nathan Altshiller. *College Geometry.* New York: Barnes & Noble, 1952.
8. Coxeter, Harold Scott Macdonald. *Introduction to Geometry.* New York: John Wiley & Sons, 1961.
9. Emch, Arnold. "Rare Problems in Plane Geometry." *Scripta Mathematica* 16 (1914):64.
10. Kostovskii, Aleksandr Nikitich. *Geometrical Constructions Using Compasses Only.* Translated from the Russian by Halina Moss. New York: Pergamon Press, 1961.
11. Kutuzov, B. V. *Geometry.* Studies in Mathematics, vol. 4. Translated by Louis I. Gordon and Edward S. Shater. (Distributed by SMSG.) Chicago: University of Chicago, 1960.
12. Pedoe, Daniel. *Circles.* New York: Pergamon Press, 1957.
13. Steiner, Jakob. *Geometrical Constructions with a Ruler.* Translated from the German by Marion Elizabeth Stark. New York: Scripta Mathematica, 1950.
14. Taylor, E. H., and Grover C. Bartoo. *An Introduction to College Geometry.* Hastings, Mich.: Lithocraft, 1939.

Teacher Notes

Project 1

Method A

a) Construction. On a working line *AX*, construct *AD* = *OP* and *DB* = *k*. On another line *AY*, construct *AE* = *k*. Draw *DE* and construct *BC* parallel to *DE*. (This produces the relationship $OP/k = k/OP'$, or $OP * OP' = k^2$.) *EC* is the required line; that is, *EC* = *OP'*.

b) Solution. Draw a circle of inversion, with center *O* and radius *k*. Draw a line through *O* and construct length *OP*. Extend the line as needed and construct *OP'* on this line. Points *P* and *P'* are the desired inverse points.

c) Sketch of the solution:

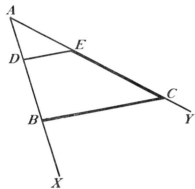

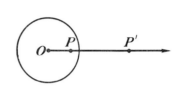

Fourth-proportional construction

Inverse point location

Method B

a) Construction. Draw a circle *A* with some radius *AB*. Mark the point *B* on the circle. At *B* construct a line of length *k* that is perpendicular to *AB*, calling it *BC*. Using point *C* as center and radius *OP*, intersect circle *A* at points *D* and *D'*. Draw line *CD* to intersect the circle at point *E*. The entire secant, *CE*, is the desired length *OP'*. (The tangent is the mean proportional between the secant and its external segment, so $CD/BC = BC/CE$, or $OP/k = k/OP'$. This satisfies the definition $OP * OP' = k^2$, and *P* and *P'* will be inverse points.)

b) Solution same as for Method A.

c) Sketch of the solution:

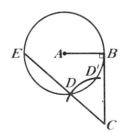

(Same as Method A)

Tangent and secant construction

Inverse point location

Method C, Case 1

a) Construction as directed

b) Sketch of the solution:

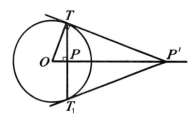

c) Analysis of deductive proof: $P'T$ is perpendicular to OT by definition of tangent lines. Hence, triangle OTP' is a right triangle with altitude TP. It follows that $OP/OT = OT/OP'$ (the leg of a right triangle is the mean proportional between the hypotenuse and the segment of the hypotenuse adjacent to the leg), or $OP * OP' = k^2$, and points P and P' are inverse points.

Method C, Case 2

    a) Construction as directed

    b) Sketch of the solution:

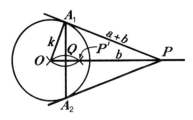

c) Analysis of deductive proof: The method used to locate point P' by using radii OA_1 and OA_2 is the construction that determines the perpendicular bisector of a line. The Pythagorean theorem may be used on the resulting right triangles OA_1Q and A_1QP. Line $OA_1 = A_1P' = k$, and $A_1P = OP$ by construction. Letting $a = OP'$ and $b = PP'$ and applying the Pythagorean theorem, we see that $k^2 = a^2/4 + A_1Q^2$ and $(a + b)^2 = A_1Q^2 + (b + a/2)^2$. From these relationships, by substitution, it follows that $(a + b)^2 = k^2 - a^2/4 + (b + a/2)^2$. This simplifies to $a^2 + ab = k^2$, which by a factorization is $a * (a + b) = k^2$, or $OP * OP' = k^2$. Hence P and P' are the required inverse points.

Project 2

Sketch of the solution:

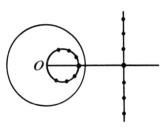

    Theorem statement. The inverse of a circle through the center of inversion is a straight line not through the center of inversion.

Project 3

Description	Sketch
1. The circle of inversion	

2. *a)* A point outside the circle

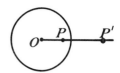

b) A point inside the circle

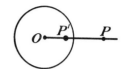

c) No inverse

3. *a)* The same line through the center

b) A circle inside and through the pole of inversion

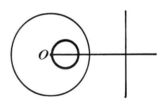

c) A circle passing through the pole and the points of intersection of the given line and the circle of inversion

4. *a)* A circle outside the circle of inversion

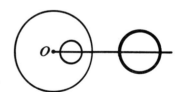

b) A circle inside

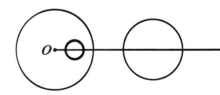

c) A circle inside and tangent to the circle of inversion

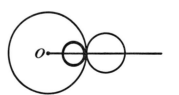

5. *a)* A line also tangent to circle of inversion

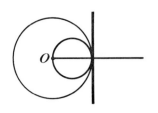

b) A line outside

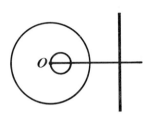

c) A line intersecting at the same two points

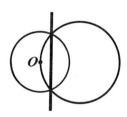

6. Another circle, concentric and outside

7. A circle concentric with and inside circle of inversion

Project 4

Description   Sketch

1. Two circles passing through pole

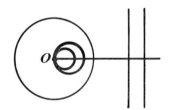

2. A family of circles through the pole

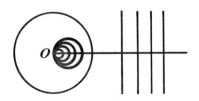

3. A line not through the pole and a circle tangent to that line, but the circle also passes through the pole

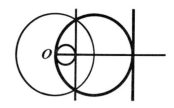

4. The same line and circle, each inverting into the other

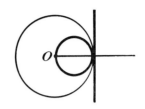

5. Two parallel lines, located on opposite sides of O

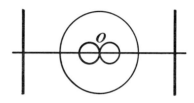

6. Two other tangent circles, located outside the circle of inversion

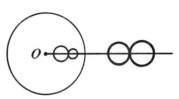

7. Exact opposite of previous exercise.

Project 5

Sketch of the construction:

1. Bisector of a line

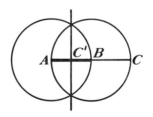

Proof

$AC' * AC = AB^2$

$AC' * 2AB = AB^2$

$2AC' = AB$

2. Locating the center of a circle

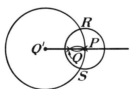

Project 6

Analysis of deductive proof: Since the diagonals of a rhombus are perpendicular bisectors of each other, $OD^2 = DE^2 + OE^2$ and $CD^2 = DE^2 + EC^2$, by application of the Pythagorean theorem. Since the sides of a rhombus are congruent, we have $AD^2 = DE^2 + EC^2$. By subtraction, $OD^2 - AD^2 = OE^2 - EC^2$. By factoring, $OD^2 - AD^2 = (OE - EC) * (EO + EC) = (OE - AE) * (OE + CE)$. This gives the desired result, $OD^2 - CD^2 = OA * OC$.

Students should turn in the homemade Peaucellier inversor along with the curve traced by use of the instrument. The inverse curve thus obtained should be similar to the line *l* sketched below.

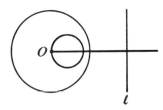

Project 7

Sketch of the inverse curves:

1.

2.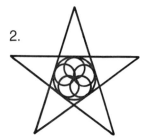

3.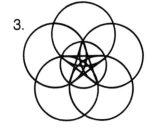

Further Investigations

Using a radius of inversion equal to one and one-half squares and placing the center of inversion at the exact center of one of the squares will yield the type of transformation shown. This transformation is shown by giving the interior of the circle only in figure 4 and including the outside in the enlargement given in figure 5.

Fig. 4

Fig. 5

The Mathematics of Flight

CESAR G. QUEYQUEP

THE flight of a bird, an insect, or a machine has always intrigued the human mind. From the mythical Daedalus and Icarus soaring into the air on wings of wax, to Leonardo da Vinci's flapping ornithopter, to the Kitty Hawk flying machine of Orville and Wilbur Wright, to today's jet airliners and fortresses of the sky, flight and its fantastic possibilities has fired the imagination of scholars, engineers, and scientists.

The centuries between Aristotle (384–322 B.C.) and Galileo (1564–1642) and Newton (1642–1727) reveal little achievement in aerodynamics. Aristotle's pupil, Alexander the Great (356–323 B.C.), is said to have flown by harnessing two strong eagles that had been starved for three days and tied to a yoke. He sat on the yoke holding a spear with a large lump of liver on its tip. Alexander supposedly made the eagles fly by holding the baited spear in front of the hungry birds.

It would be gratifying to be able to explain to other people in simple, understandable terms and computations how the flight of a heavier-than-air machine is made possible. What makes an airplane fly, how its flight path can be directed and controlled, and how it can take off and land—these are topics of interest to both young and old. Most people know that flight is a marvelous scientific achievement, but it is difficult to fully understand the mechanics of flight, much less how birds or airplanes fly and navigate the atmosphere.

The purpose of your work in the field of elementary aerodynamics is to gain knowledge about the principles of flight and try to understand, with the help of mathematics, the many aspects of heavier-than-air machine flight.

The role of mathematics in aerodynamics is very significant. The human race could not have moved beyond earthbound life to explore the realms beyond were it not for a knowledge of calculus and differential equations.

In this work, you will see how mathematics contributes to the understanding of airplane flight. You will use mathematics up to the calculus to do the following:

1. Predict airplane performance
2. Calculate propeller thrust and jet engine thrust
3. Explain propeller theory and characteristics
4. Calculate the lift, drag, and other forces acting on the airplane

Projects

Project 1: Highlights in Aviation History

Trace the history of airplane flight. Find out what contributions to achieving human flight were made by many of the world's thinkers and inventors. Include the following pioneers in powered flight: Leonardo da Vinci, Sir George Cayley, John Stringfellow, Clement Ader, Sir Hiram Maxim, Samuel Pierpont Langley, J. M. Le Bris, Luis Mouillard, Otto Lilienthal, and Wilbur and Orville Wright.

Draw or sketch on 8½″ × 11″ typewriting paper Leonardo da Vinci's ornithopter and the Wright brothers' flying machine or Samuel Langley's "Aerodrome." Use one sheet for each drawing. Use pencil first and then go over your lines with black pen. Be sure to label the figures. References 1, 2, 3, 8, and 10 will help you.

Guide: It is enough for you to know what each of these men did, what models they built, or what experiments they performed. If mathematics calculations were used in their designs, these may be mentioned, but experimental data and computations can be omitted. For example, you could mention that Leonardo da Vinci was among the first to build a birdlike machine late in the fifteenth century. It was a crude contrivance designed to sustain itself in flight by a flapping wing operated by the pilot.

It may be a good idea to build an airplane model of your own original design while working on the requirements of this project. Balsa wood, model airplane glue, tissue frame covers, and other needed parts can be purchased inexpensively at hobby stores. The model can subsequently be used to demonstrate the components of the airplane and its positions while turning about its longitudinal axis, horizontal axis, and the vertical axis.

Project 2: Basic Components of the Airplane

On 18″ × 24″ posterboard, draw either three views of an airplane—a front view, right side view, and top view—or draw a single pictorial (isometric or oblique) view. Label the parts and learn the main function of each. Tell what each part does to keep the airplane aloft, pull it forward through the atmosphere, turn it left or right, or take off and land on the ground or at sea.

Guide: Identify the following basic components of an airplane and learn their functions: power plant (engine), cockpit or cabin, wing, fuselage, rudder, horizontal tail, vertical tail, landing gear, elevator, ailerons, and flaps. References 3, 4, 14, and 15 will be helpful. You may wish to use this drawing later if you are asked to talk about your project to Boy Scout groups, junior air scout squadrons, or other air-minded clubs or groups in the community. In some places, model airplane competitions are held annually by Boy Scouts, air scouts, and model airplane hobbyists and enthusiasts.

Project 3: How Lift Is Created and Measured

Write an explanation of how lift (the lifting force on the wing) is created by the wings of the airplane. How is it calculated?

Guide: To complete this project, it is necessary to understand two theories on the creation of lift, namely momentum theory and pressure theory.

1. *Momentum theory:* Discuss the momentum theory and include diagrams, drawings, and calculations for impulse and momentum.

2. *Pressure theory:* Investigate the equation of continuity, Bernoulli's equation, and the application of Bernoulli's equation on incompressible fluid flow. (Note that Bernoulli's equation is applicable not only to incompressible fluids but also to air—provided that the velocity of air flow is well below the speed of sound). Also show the formula for determining lift. Include diagrams or tables and charts used for evaluating the lift coefficient C_L and the magnitude of the lift L itself.

Summarizing Project 3, the following equations, figures, charts, and graphs are needed.

Equations
- Momentum equation
- Impulse equation
- Continuity principle, or continuity equation
- Lift coefficient equation
- Formula for lift on an airplane wing

Figures, drawings, charts
- Figure to illustrate the continuity principle
- Illustration of the Venturi tube
- Air flow around an airfoil (airplane wing)
- Aerodynamic characteristics of an airfoil

Use References 4, 13, 14, and 15, or any other book you can find on aerodynamics.

Project 4: Aerodynamic Drag on the Airplane

Explain how air resistance (or drag) on an airplane in flight is determined.

Guide: To complete this project, it is necessary to do the following.

1. Define and explain the terms below; include formulas and calculations, if any.

a) Profile drag: what it is and what causes it

b) Induced drag: why it is called induced drag and why it occurs

c) Parasite drag: how it is estimated

d) Total drag

2. Reproduce the chart or charts containing the coefficient for profile and induced drag from the references cited below. Use References 4, 13, 14, and 15 (fig. 3.4, p. 114).

Project 5: Aircraft Propulsion

Explain the following:

1. The forces acting on a blade element of an aircraft propeller using the blade element theory. Draw (a) a propeller blade showing an element and (b) a diagram showing the forces acting on the blade element.

2. The thrust and torque forces acting on the propeller

3. The thrust derived by propellers

4. Jet propulsion theory and the calculation of jet engine thrust

Guide: Airplanes derive propulsion from either propeller or jet engine thrust. These planes belong to the powered-aircraft group. Gliders are heavier-than-air machines that fly without power plants and derive lift from thermal currents in the atmosphere. The equations and figures needed for this project follow.

Equations

- Resultant air velocity striking any element of the propeller blade at radius r
- Equations for thrust and torque components
- Work done by thrust force
- Efficiency of blade element
- Propulsion efficiency of a jet engine
- Thrust or propulsion force of a jet engine

Figures, drawings, charts, and graphs

- Figure showing a propeller blade and an element of the blade
- Forces acting on a propeller blade
- Figure showing relative air velocities in propeller and jet propulsion

Project 6: Equilibrium and Performance

Identify the forces acting on an airplane in level flight, a climb, or a dive. Show how to determine such aspects of performance as rate of climb, absolute ceiling, endurance, and range.

Guide: The airplane is subjected to a number of forces in flight. As it changes positions from level flight to a climb or dive, there are variations on the effect of these forces on the aircraft. The ability of the aircraft to maintain equilibrium under these changing conditions is a test of its stability. An airplane's performance is evaluated generally in terms of its maneuverability, stability, rate of climb, endurance range, and absolute ceiling.

Equations needed

- Equilibrium in level flight
- Equilibrium in a climb and a dive
- Calculating rate of climb
- Fuel consumed per unit increase in altitude
- Range

Figures, charts, and graphs needed

- Figures showing forces acting on the plane in level flight with angle of attack positive and angle of attack negative

- Equilibrium in a climb
- Equilibrium in a dive
- Graph for calculating absolute ceiling

REFERENCES

1. Andrews, Allen. *The Flying Machine: Its Evolution through the Ages.* New York: G. P. Putnam's Sons, 1977.
2. Ahnstrom, Doris M. *The Complete Book of Helicopters.* Cleveland: World Publishing Co., 1954.
3. Benton, William. *Encyclopaedia Britannica.* 14th ed., s.v. "Aircraft Propulsion."
4. Diehl, Walter S. *Engineering Aerodynamics.* New York: Ronald Press Co., 1928.
5. Durand, William F. *Aerodynamic Theory.* Berlin: Verlag Julius Springer, 1935.
6. Etkin, Bernard. *Dynamics of Atmospheric Flight.* New York: John Wiley & Sons, 1972.
7. Etkin, Bernard. *Dynamics of Flight.* New York: John Wiley & Sons, 1959.
8. Gibbs-Smith, Charles H. *A History of Flying.* New York: Frederick A. Praeger, 1954.
9. Miele, Angelo. *Flight Mechanics.* Vol. 1. Reading, Mass.: Addison-Wesley Publishing Co., 1962.
10. Miller, Francis Trevelyan. *The World in the Air.* New York: Putnam, 1930.
11. Pope, Alan, and John J. Harper. *Low-Speed Wind Tunnel Testing.* New York: John Wiley & Sons, 1966.
12. Sutton, Oliver G. *The Science of Flight.* Baltimore: Penguin Books, 1949.
13. Talay, Theodore A. *Introduction to the Aerodynamics of Flight.* NASA SP-367. Washington, D.C.: National Aeronautics and Space Administration, 1975.
14. Weast, Robert C., and Melvin J. Astle. *CRC Handbook of Chemistry and Physics.* Boca Raton, Fla.: CRC Press, 1979.
15. Wood, Karl D. *Technical Aerodynamics.* New York: McGraw-Hill Book Co., 1947.
16. Zemansky, Mark W., Francis W. Sears, and Hugh D. Young. *University Physics.* Reading, Mass.: Addison-Wesley Publishing Co., 1980.

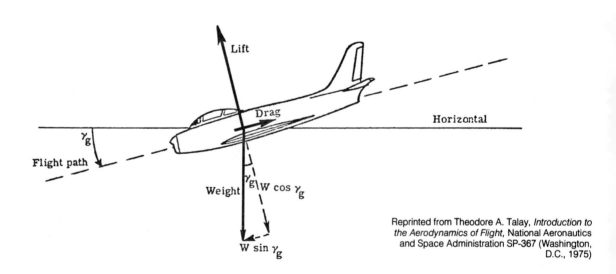

Reprinted from Theodore A. Talay, *Introduction to the Aerodynamics of Flight,* National Aeronautics and Space Administration SP-367 (Washington, D.C., 1975)

Teacher Notes

Project 1

Leonardo da Vinci: Born in Tuscany, Italy, Leonardo da Vinci was a fifteenth-century painter, sculptor, and mechanical genius of great fame. His idea of an ornithopter, a flapping-wing contrivance, was among the earliest attempts to imitate the bird in flight (see fig. 1). The device was supposed to operate by a system of pulleys that the pilot powered himself. The mechanical difficulties, however, were so numerous that the machine did not even have a small amount of success.

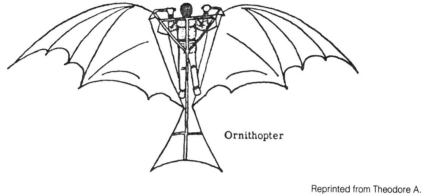

Ornithopter

Reprinted from Theodore A. Talay, *Introduction to the Aerodynamics of Flight,* National Aeronautics and Space Administration SP-367 (Washington, D.C., 1975)

Fig. 1. Leonardo da Vinci's ornithopter design

Sir George Cayley: In 1796, Sir George Cayley made a working model of a helicopter. In fact, the helicopter is recognized as the earliest invented form of heavier-than-air machines. A model for the helicopter was invented in the mid-fifteenth century by the Chinese, who called it the "Chinese top." The Chinese flying top used rotating feathers to fly upward into the air. George Cayley used a spool with a string around it for his "engine." When he pulled the string, the spool revolved, spinning the blades very fast till up it went, climbing as the blades whirled. Cayley's model rose sixty feet off the ground, but he soon realized that if it had to carry people aloft, there had to be a light but powerful "engine," which, of course, had not yet been invented. He therefore had to abandon his idea of a spiral wing. From 1799 to 1810, he worked on a fixed-wing glider and succeeded in 1853 in building a glider in which his coachman flew successfully.

John Stringfellow: Stringfellow made improvements on glider design in 1868 by putting camber, or curvature, into the wings of the craft. He discovered that a cambered wing creates a greater lifting force than a flat one because the camber creates a positive pressure on the underside of the wing and a negative pressure on the upper surface. The difference in pressure produces the lifting effect.

Clement Ader: Ader designed an airplane that was supposed to fly on steam power. Although he claimed that he was the first man to take off in an airplane by its own power, his "Avion III" failed to rise off the ground in a test in 1897.

Sir Hiram Maxim: Maxim experimented extensively on air resistance and on propulsion problems, beginning in 1894. One of his designs was a monoplane powered by steam, using a railway track for take-off. It was wrecked during a take-off and could not get off the ground.

Samuel Pierpont Langley: Langley is known as one of the great experimenters in aviation and was a secretary of the Smithsonian Institution in Washington, D.C. In 1896, he built models of airplanes, which he called "aerodromes" (see fig. 2). One of these models flew for about 4000 feet in a circular path. This encouraged him to build full-sized models powered with light gasoline engines. His two attempts to launch these machines from houseboats on the Potomac River failed.

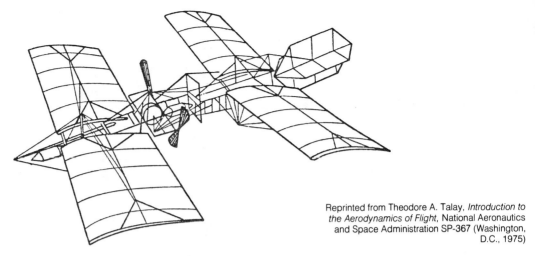

Reprinted from Theodore A. Talay, *Introduction to the Aerodynamics of Flight,* National Aeronautics and Space Administration SP-367 (Washington, D.C., 1975)

Fig. 2. Samuel Langley's aerodrome

Le Bris: Le Bris was a sea captain. He built a man-carrying glider in the shape of an albatross in 1856; gasoline engines were not yet available, so experimenters resorted to gliding contrivances. Le Bris launched a number of glider models, but none flew successfully.

Mouillard: Mouillard designed and built a glider plane in Algiers in about 1865. He attempted to fly the aircraft but had many mechanical difficulties. Mouillard published the results of his experiments in his book *L'Empire de l'Air.*

Lilienthal: Born in Prussia and trained at the Berlin Trade Academy, Otto Lilienthal was among the world's great aeronautical pioneers. He experimented with flapping wings and gliders, wrote a book on the flight of birds, and made several hundred flights in gliders. He was killed when his glider turned over in a tragic flight in 1896.

Wilbur and Orville Wright: These two brothers from Dayton, Ohio, made the first controlled and sustained powered flight in a heavier-than-air machine at Kitty Hawk, North Carolina, in 1903. They had first built huge kites and then gliders, before designing their powered aircraft.

They constructed a lightweight twelve-horsepower gasoline engine, then installed it in one of their gliders and called the machine the Flyer.

In its first test flight, the airplane was airborne for only twelve seconds. In a subsequent trial flight at Kitty Hawk, after some revisions and refinements in the control system were made, the airplane flew for almost a minute and covered nearly one-half a mile. That flight marked the dawn of a new era in which heavier-than-air machines would revolutionize economic, political, and social trends.

Project 2: **Basic Components of an Airplane** (See fig. 3)

Power plant: The power plant, or engine, produces the power to move the plane forward. Until nearly the end of World War II in 1945, most airplanes were propeller driven by gasoline engines. The engines turned propellers that either pulled or pushed the airplane forward. Gasoline engines with driving propellers are still in use on small airplanes used for sports or short-distance travel and in agriculture for spraying insecticides on plants and trees. Jet engines are used for commercial airliners and modern military aircraft.

Cockpit: the cockpit, or cabin, houses the instruments and control levers used by the pilot to direct the plane along the desired flight path.

Fuselage: The fuselage is the longitudinal portion of the plane used for cargo and passengers.

Wing: The wing is the only part of the airplane that produces *lift* —the force that sustains the airplane in the air. Monoplanes have a single set of wings, biplanes have two sets, and triplanes have three. The wings have *camber,* a curvature upward in the middle that promotes a greater difference in air pressure between the upper and lower surfaces. This difference products lift.

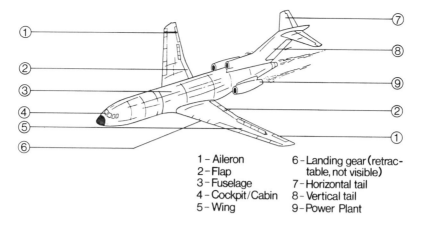

1 – Aileron	6 – Landing gear (retrac-
2 – Flap	table, not visible)
3 – Fuselage	7 – Horizontal tail
4 – Cockpit/Cabin	8 – Vertical tail
5 – Wing	9 – Power Plant

Fig. 3. Basic components of the airplane

Reprinted from Theodore A. Talay, *Introduction to the Aerodynamics of Flight*, National Aeronautics and Space Administration SP-367 (Washington, D.C., 1975)

Horizontal tail: The horizontal tail section consists of the fixed horizontal stabilizer and the movable elevator. The horizontal stabilizer provides directional stability along the x-axis, enabling the aircraft to return to its horizontal position when necessary. The elevator produces the *pitching* movement of the plane, causing the plane either to climb or to dive when the pilot uses it to control altitude.

Vertical tail: The vertical tail section consists of the fixed vertical fin and the movable rudder. The vertical fin provides directional stability along the y-axis, enabling the aircraft to return to its vertical position when necessary. The rudder provides a way to control the vertical direction of flight. Without a rudder, an airplane cannot turn smoothly left or right. This left or right motion along the vertial axis is called *yaw.*

Landing gear: The landing gear system consists of the main wheels and a tail or nose wheel. It is used for takeoff and landing. In seaplanes, the wheels are replaced with *pontoons,* or floats, capable of buoying the entire aircraft on the surface of the water.

Ailerons: These are the movable portions of the wings located at the rear, or trailing edge, and close to each wing tip. When actuated by the pilot, the ailerons move simultaneously but not in the same direction; when the aileron on the right wing goes up the one on the left wing goes down, and vice versa. Ailerons cause the airplane to turn along the longitudinal axis, parallel to the fuselage, in a motion called *roll.*

Flaps: Flaps are movable, high-lift devices located on the trailing edge of each wing and closest to the fuselage. Unlike ailerons, flaps move simultaneously in the same direction: down. Flaps are used to change the orientation of the wing, or angle of attack, with respect to the direction of the airstream over the wing. When landing, an airplane must decrease its velocity. To make up for this decreased velocity, the angle of attack must be increased in order to increase the lift coefficient and the decreasing lift on the plane itself.

Project 3: How Lift Is Created and Measured

Lift is the force that supports an airplane in flight. It is produced by the reaction of air on a wing. Some theories regarding the creation of lift are these:

1. *Momentum Theory:* The atmosphere is, for the most part, filled with air. Like other forms of matter, air is composed of particles that are free to move and occupy space. In actual flight, the air surrounding the wing is usually thought of as being a region of still air with the wing moving through it.

What happens is made clearer by experiments in a wind tunnel, a device for testing aircraft design models. In these tests, the wing remains stationary while the surrounding air is made to move at a designated velocity. These moving particles of air have momentum. In equation form,

(1)
$$M = m \cdot v$$

where M = momentum in ft lbs/sec, *m* = mass of air flying past the wing per unit time in lbs, and *v* = velocity of the moving air in ft/sec.

This momentum, when opposed, is reduced to zero. In the process of being reduced to zero, the momentum creates a certain amount of impulse. The derived impulse J is

(2)
$$J = F \cdot t$$

where F = force in lbs and t = time in seconds. The force F acts on the wing and sustains the airplane in flight. F acts on the wing in t units of time, long enough to keep the wing, and therefore the airplane, airborne.

2. *Pressure theory:* This theory has as its underlying principle the famous Bernoulli equation. The Bernoulli equation has as its basis the equation of continuity. To understand the equation of continuity, consider a stationary, closed surface in a moving fluid. The fluid flows into the volume enclosed by the surface at some points and flows out at others.

Referring to figure 4, if A_1 is the cross-section of a fluid at one point in a tube of flow, and A_2 is the cross-section of the fluid at another point, and V_1 and V_2 are the fluid velocities at these points, the fluid mass across A_1 and A_2 during time dt is constant.

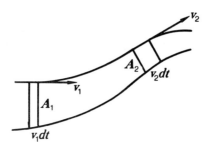

Fig. 4. Flow into and out of a tube of flow

Since the flow is steady, the mass flowing in is equal to the mass flowing out. That is,

(3)
$$\rho A_1 V_1 dt = \rho A_2 V_2 dt.$$

The upward pressure on the undersurface of a wing is greater than the downward pressure on the upper surface of a wing. The net force is called lift.

How lift is measured: The amount of lift on a wing depends on the wing's angle of attack—the angle that its lower surface forms with the direction of the airstream. The aerodynamic characteristics of a wing or airfoil are understood by wind tunnel tests. One of these characteristics is the lift coefficient C_L, gained by measuring the lift force per unit length of the wing and nondimensionalizing as follows:

(4)
$$C_L = \frac{L}{q^c}$$

where L = the lift, measured per unit length of the wing, q = the testing dynamic pressure, or $\frac{1}{2}\rho V^2$, C = the chord length of the airfoil, and ρ = the mass density of the air.

Figure 5 demonstrates the equation of continuity, the basis of the Bernoulli equation as applied to a Venturi tube. Note from the fluid levels in the two tubes that at the constricted portion of the tubes the pressure is less than in the regions both ahead of and behind the constriction. From the equation of continuity, we know that speed V_2 is greater than speed V_1, and therefore pressure P_2 in the throat is less than pressure P_1. Air is drawn into the low pressure fluid rushing through the constriction. The setup is called a Venturi meter.

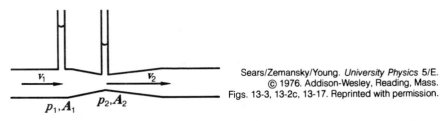

Fig. 5. The Venturi tube

Figure 6 shows the flow of air around a section of an airfoil. The orientation of the wing relative to the direction of the airstream causes the flow lines of the air to crowd together at the upper wing surface. This situation is much similar to the throat, or constricted portion, of the Venturi tube.

Fig. 6. Air flow around a wing section, or airfoil

The region above the wing is therefore a region of reduced pressure, and the region below the wing is a region of increased pressure. The upward lift is determined by the formula

(5)
$$L = C_L \frac{\rho}{2}AV^2$$

where C_L = lift coefficient, ρ = mass density of the air in slugs/ft³, A = area of the wing, and V = velocity of the air in ft/sec. As mentioned earlier, the lift coefficient is determined by wind tunnel tests. Figure 7 is a graph of C_L and other aerodynamic characteristics plotted against the angle of attack.

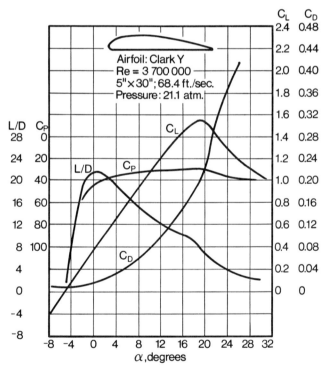

Fig. 7. Characteristics of an airfoil with aspect ratio 6

As the angle of attack is increased from zero, the graph shows that lift increases linearly with the angle. The limit beyond which lift does not increase as the angle of attack changes is known as the *stalling angle*. At this angle, no lift is created and the airplane starts to fall.

Project 4: Aerodynamic Drag on the Airplane

Drag is the total resistance of the air to an airplane as it moves through the atmosphere. Any object traveling through the air encounters a resistance because air is a viscous fluid. Like water, it tends to stick to all matter moving through it.

a) *Profile drag* is the resistance offered by the air because of its viscosity. Profile drag is directly proportional to the coefficient of drag, C_D, another of the airfoil characteristics. It is computed in the same way as lift equation 5. The formula for drag is

(6)
$$\text{Drag} = C_D\, \frac{\rho}{2}\, AV^2$$

where C_D = the drag coefficient and ρ = the mass density of the air in slugs / ft³, and V = air velocity in ft/sec. Refer again to figure 7 for the value of the drag coefficient C_D. Note that, like the lift coefficient C_L, C_D varies also with the angle of attack.

b) *Induced drag* is the resistance of the surrounding air that develops when lift is generated by the wings. This resistance, which is necessary, results from the creation of lift. The induced drag is given by the relation

(7)
$$D_i = C_{D_i}\, \frac{\rho}{2}\, AV^2$$

where C_{D_i} = coefficient of induced drag in lbs, ρ = mass density of the air in slugs/ft³, and V = velocity in ft/sec. However, the coefficient C_{D_i} is not available from the graph. Its value is obtained from the C_L by the formula

(8)
$$C_{D_i} = \frac{C_L{}^2}{\pi AR}$$

The symbol *AR* stands for aspect ratio, which is obtained by dividing span by the chord.

(9)
$$AR = \frac{\text{span}}{\text{chord}} \text{ or } \frac{\text{span}^2}{\text{wing area}}$$

c) *Parasite drag* refers to the air resistance on parts of an airplane other than the wings. Some of the affected parts are the fuselage, tail surfaces, engine nacelles, landing gear, wing tanks, and engine(s).

There is no standard formula for computing parasite drag for component parts because these parts differ in form and size from one airplane to another. However, the references cited in this requirement give examples on how to estimate the parasite drag by finding the equivalent flat plate areas of the components.

d) *Total drag* is not merely the sum of the drag of an airplane's components. When these components are combined together, one part can affect the flow field, and consequently the drag of another component. This kind of drag is termed *interference drag*. For rough computational purposes, interference drag is about 5 to 10 percent of the total airplane drag.

Project 5: Aircraft Propulsion

Propellers can have two blades or four. Consider figure 8, a blade element of a propeller.

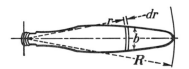

Fig. 8. Blade element *dr* of a propeller

Picture the propeller as composed of these small blade elements, each of which resembles the shape of a wing section (airfoil). The resultant velocity created by air striking any blade element at radius *r* at an angle with the plane of rotation given by the relation

NCTM Projects to Enrich School Mathematics: Level 3

(10)
$$\tan \phi = \frac{V}{2\pi rn}$$

is indicated in figure 9.

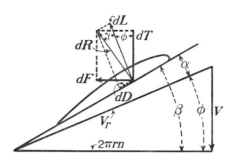

Fig. 9. Forces acting on a blade element of a propeller

(11)
$$\tan \gamma = \frac{D}{L},$$

where L = lift

(12)
$$dL = C_L \frac{\rho}{2} \, dr \, V_r^2,$$

where C_L = lift coefficient;

(13)
$$dR = C_1 \frac{\rho}{2} b dr V_r^2,$$

where ρ = mass density, dr = element of radius r, and V_r = velocity of the element at radius r.
   The thrust and torque components of force are

(14)
$$dT = dR \cos(\phi + \gamma)$$

and

(15)
$$dF = dR \sin(\phi + \gamma).$$

Work per second accomplished by the force of the thrust on the blade element is

(16)
$$W_T = V \, dT.$$

Work per second accomplished against the force *dF is*

(17)
$$W_{dF} = 2\pi rn dF.$$

The efficiency of the blade element is

(18)
$$\eta_e = \frac{V dR \cos(\phi + \gamma)}{2\pi rn dR \sin(\phi + \gamma)},$$

but

(19)
$$\frac{V}{2\pi rn} = \tan \phi;$$

so

(20)
$$\eta_e = \frac{\tan \phi}{\tan(\phi + \gamma)}.$$

   The underlying principle of the blade element theory is that propeller blades, in their motion through a fluid, exert a force dependent on the airfoil-like shape of the blade elements. The propeller is composed of a number of blade elements along the radius that function as small airfoils or wing sections. The theory was initated by William Froude in 1878 but owes its development to the work of S. Drzewiecki and finds its complete expression in his book *Théorie Générale de Phélice* (Paris, 1920).

Calculation of thrust: The thrust can be calculated by integrating the differential equation of the thrust component of force (equation 14).

Jet propulsion: In figure 10, the power P_i required to increase the velocity of the air from V to V_j is

(21)
$$P_i = \frac{m}{2g_o}(V_j^2 - V^2)$$

where m = mass of air flow per unit time, g_o = the proportionality constant, V_j = air velocity behind engine and V = air velocity as it approaches engine. The power needed to propel the plane from V to V_j is

(22)
$$P_p = TV = \left[\frac{m}{g_o}(V_j - V) \right] \cdot V.$$

The propulsion efficiency E_p is the ratio of P_i and P_p.

(23)
$$E_p = \frac{P_p}{P_i} = \frac{\dfrac{m}{g_o}(V \cdot V_j - V^2)}{\dfrac{m}{2g_o}(V_j^2 - V^2)}$$

(24)
$$= \frac{2}{\dfrac{V_j}{V} + 1}$$

E_p is known as the Froude efficiency after R. E. Froude who, with W. M. Rankine, developed the theory.

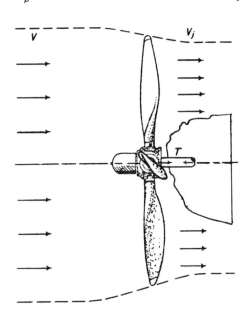

Fig. 10. Velocities of air flow in front of and behind the propeller (left), and in front of and behind the jet engine (below).

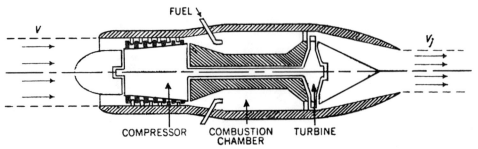

The propulsion force, or thrust, T, is

(25)
$$T = \frac{m}{g_o}(V_j - V).$$

Equation 25 is based on Newton's second law of motion, which also applies to propeller thrust.

NCTM Projects to Enrich School Mathematics: Level 3

Project 6: Forces in Flight—Performance

1. *Straight or level flight:* α = angle of attack = O. To provide the needed lift, α must be positive (although in some cases, slightly negative) since the airplane is moving relatively slowly; C_L increases directly as α until the stalling limit is reached. Hence, L varies directly as the square of velocity V. It is easily seen that in level flight (fig. 11 and 12)

(26) $$T = D$$

and

(27) $$L = W$$

where L = lift, D = drag, T = thrust, and W = weight.

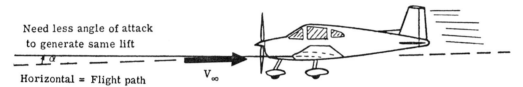

Reprinted from Theodore A. Talay, *Introduction to the Aerodynamics of Flight,* National Aeronautics and Space Administration SP-367 (Washington, D.C., 1975)

Fig. 11. Horizontal (level) flight, showing angle of attack greater than O, and less than O.

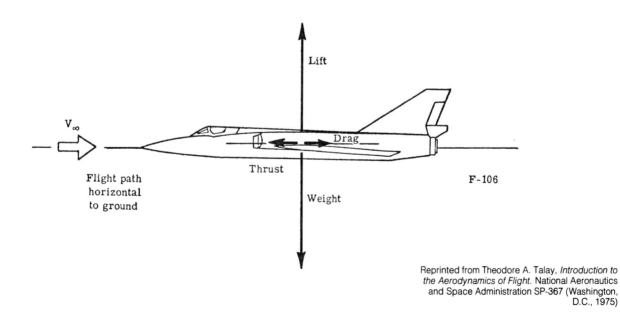

Reprinted from Theodore A. Talay, *Introduction to the Aerodynamics of Flight.* National Aeronautics and Space Administration SP-367 (Washington, D.C., 1975)

Fig. 12. Forces in equilibrium during horizontal (level) flight

2. Unaccelerated straight climb: In a climb (fig. 13)

(28)
$$L = W \cos \gamma$$

and

(29)
$$T = D + W \sin \gamma.$$

To maintain a straight climbing path, the lift should be equal to the weight component perpendicular to the flight path.

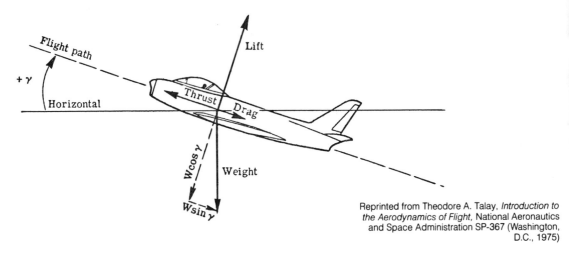

Reprinted from Theodore A. Talay, *Introduction to the Aerodynamics of Flight*, National Aeronautics and Space Administration SP-367 (Washington, D.C., 1975)

Fig. 13. Forces acting on the airplane during a climb.

In a dive (fig. 14)

(30)
$$T = D + W \sin (-\gamma)$$
$$= D - W \sin \gamma$$

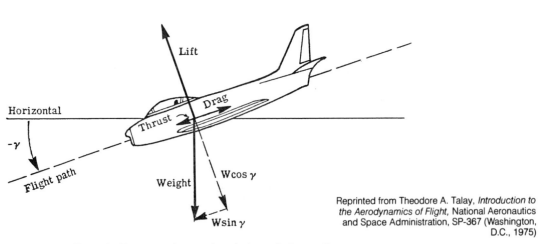

Reprinted from Theodore A. Talay, *Introduction to the Aerodynamics of Flight*, National Aeronautics and Space Administration, SP-367 (Washington, D.C., 1975)

Fig. 14. Forces acting on the airplane during a dive

It should be noted that in a dive the component of the weight along the flight path helps provide thrust by reducing the drag component for constant velocity.

3. *Rate of climb:* The rate of climb and the fuel consumed per unit increase in altitude are given by the relations

(31)
$$C = \frac{[T(h, V, \pi) - D(h, V, W)]V}{W}$$

(32)
$$-\frac{dW}{dh} = \frac{q(h, V,)W}{[T(h, V, \pi) - D(h, V, W)]V} ,$$

where $q = cT$ is the fuel consumed per unit time, $T - D$ = the excess thrust per unit weight, and $TV - DV$ = the excess horsepower (power available − the power needed to overcome aerodynamic drag). Thus, the rate of climb is equal to the excess HP (horsepower) per unit weight. In figure 15, the lines sloping downward indicate the values of HP available (dropping as altitude increases). The curves sloping to the right indicate minimum power required, which increases with altitude also. The absolute ceiling is the intersection of Pro/Pao with the power available curve.

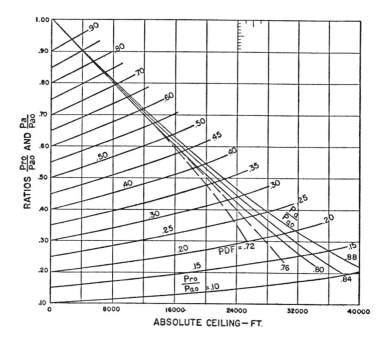

Fig. 15. Absolute ceiling chart for a fixed pitch propeller

4. *Endurance:* Endurance is the length of flight time possible with the maximum fuel load. Endurance is obtained by dividing the fuel load by the specific fuel consumption and actual brake horsepower of the engine.

5. *Range:* The range is the maximum distance the plane could travel under a maximum fuel load. The range R at maximum speed is

(33)
$$R = E_o \cdot V_M$$

where E_o = endurance at maximum speed and V_M = maximum speed.

6. *Absolute ceiling:* The absolute ceiling is defined as the maximum altitude at which the airplane's rate of climb is zero. Since the rate of climb is zero, it is attainable theoretically only in infinite time. A ceiling can be attained only if the rate of climb at that ceiling is a positive small rate.

The calculation of the ceiling involves a graphical method. For a fixed-pitch propeller, the ceiling can be determined from the graph in figure 15.

Paradoxes in Mathematics

P. G. CASAZZA

PARADOXES and riddles have played a significant role in motivating students in their mathematical studies as well as intriguing and amusing people for over twenty-five hundred years. Each step in this project is designed to lead you through some of the major paradoxes in mathematics, tell you where they come from, and show you how some can be resolved whereas others cannot. Often, modern mathematicians follow similar steps in solving their problems. Just using the techniques developed here, you should be able to increase your other problem-solving skills.

Projects

Project I

Embark on your study of paradoxes by learning the definition of the word *paradox* as well as the origin of the word and its earliest known usage.

Guide: Check Reference 16; it will help you here. There are more than six different uses of the word *paradox* today. Now make a list of these and carefully consider the differences among them.

Usually the single most important reason students cannot solve math problems is that they do not fully understand what the problem is they are trying to solve. Moreover, no successful mathematicians got that way by trying to solve problems they didn't understand. Because this part of the project gives you the opportunity to learn exactly what a paradox is, "you will know one when you see one." Expand your mind. Read on.

Project II

Verify that each of the following is a paradox:

1. In a certain town there is a barber who shaves all those people, and only those people, who do not shave themselves.

2. | The statement in this box is false.

3. | 1. There are 3 statements in this box.
    2. There are 2 statements in this box.
    3. Two of the three statements in this box are false.

4. I have told you a million times—never exaggerate.

5. The statement: Every generality is false.

6. Early in his life Tristram Shandy decided to write his own autobiography. Lest he miss any important detail, he spent two years chronicling the first two days of his life. Lamentably, he realized that at this rate material would accumulate much faster than he could deal with it and that as the years went by he would be further and further from the end of his task. What he did not realize was that if he had only lived forever he could have written his entire autobiography. He could have finished the first year of his life in 365 years, the tenth year in 3650 years, and for all n, the nth year in $365n$ years (modulo leap years).

Guide: You will find other forms of paradoxes 1–5 above in References 13, 14, and 20. These paradoxes are all variations of what is known as the Liar's Paradox. Hundreds of articles and books have been written on this subject.

Example 1 is called the Barber's Paradox and is of the type devised by the famous mathematician-philosopher Bertrand Russell (see Reference 18). For your analysis, you should ask yourself the question, "Who shaves the barber?" One approach to example 3 is to recognize that of statements one and two, one is true and one is false so that statement three can be neither true nor false without producing a contradiction. Look in Reference 6 for the attempted autobiography of Tristram Shandy. Large numbers of other paradoxes can be found in References 2, 3, 4, 15, 17, and 18. Often a recent mathematical result is contained in a mathematics journal article, such as Reference 3. When you have need of such an article, you should write directly to the author and ask him or her to send you a reprint of the article (with your request send the title of the article and the date and name of the journal in which it appeared). If you do not know the author's address, go to any university mathematics department and ask for the *Combined Membership List* of the AMS/MAA (the American Mathematical Society and the Mathematical Association of America).

Now you have completed the second step followed by modern mathematicians in their work: Get as many examples as possible to help you understand your problem.

Project III

I can never lie to you. So believe me when I tell you that this project contains references to five paradoxes and one verse about paradoxes. And if you look these up in the exact order given and explain them, I guarantee that the one that is not a paradox will be a complete surprise to you.

1. **P**erhaps you have heard of Don Quixote
   And the strange land of which he loves to tell;
   Recent visitors are asked: "Why did you come here?"
   Answer truthfully, and all is well;
   Don't lie (lest they hang you immediately)
   Or say: "I came to be hanged today."
   Xenophobia just cannot be cured that way.

2. The Unexpected Hanging paradox

3. Have you heard the biblical paradox in Paul's letter to Titus, which ends, "The Cretans are always liars"?

4. Everyone should know Lewis Carroll's paradoxical discussion between Achilles and the Tortoise.

5. Now look up Zeno's paradoxes on motion.

6. Even W. S. Gilbert tried his hand at paradox with a two-liner that begins: "How quaint the ways of paradox."

Guide: *Xenophobia* is the fear of strangers. The acrostic in number 1 will make sense if you read *Don Quixote* (Reference 19) or if you look in Reference 3. See Reference 12 for a wonderfully complex acrostic entitled "Contracrostipunctus." Exercise 2 has also generated a considerable amount of literature. New light was shed on this subject by Reference 9, which contains the statement of the paradox and other references. The paradox referred to in number 3 is the original statement of the Liar's Paradox and appears in Paul's letter to Titus (see the King James version of the Bible, Titus 1:12–13). Exercise 4 refers to the famous Lewis Carroll who wrote *Alice in Wonderland*. Newman (Reference 14) reproduces this paradox in the article entitled. "What the Tortoise Said to Achilles and Other Riddles." Charles Dodgson wrote the original in his book *The Rectory Umbrella* (Reference 5). Even though the mathematics career of the Reverend Charles Lutwidge Dodgson was not a total success (despite his twenty-seven years as a lecturer at Oxford University), the fame he obtained under his pen name Lewis Carroll made up for it. You can find an analysis of Lewis Carroll's contributions to mathematics in Reference 25. Of the many paradoxes invented by Zeno (who lived from 495 B.C. to 435 B.C.), four have intrigued mathematicians to this day. Usually these are referred to as the Dichotomy, the Paradox of Achilles and the Tortoise, the Arrow Paradox, and the Paradox of the Stadium. Read all four. Even if you do not understand them, you should be able to recognize that they are paradoxical. A modern interpretation of these four paradoxes can be found in Reference 11. Different approaches to Zeno's paradoxes can be found in References 14 and 18. While doing this project you might enjoy reading the interesting accounts of Zeno's life and writings in References 1, 23, and 24.

If you have completed step 5, you should notice that you are in a paradoxical situation. Look again at the statement of this project and locate the paradox. Look for the quote of W. S. Gilbert (of "Gilbert and Sullivan" fame) in Act 2 of *The Pirates of Penzance* (Reference 10).

Becoming and being a mathematician require endless hours in the library. Each piece of information should be traced to its source to be sure of its accuracy.

Project IV

Think about the common elements of each of the groups of paradoxes listed below and make up two paradoxes of your own of each type.

A. Reread Project II, number 1, and compare it to this statement: There is a robot that repairs all those those robots, and only those robots, that do not repair themselves.

B. Use Project II, number 2, and the following paradox:

The statement in Box B is false.		The statement in Box A is true.
Box A		**Box B**

C. 1. Examine the rule, "Every rule has exceptions."
   2. Think about the statement, "All knowledge is doubtful."

D. 1. Have the examples in part C any relationship to a button that says, "Ban buttons"?
   2. Explore the possibility of obeying a sign that says, "Don't read this."

Guide: Let me mention that another important quality of mathematicians is persistence. Answers rarely come easily. Significant work may require you to look for a common thread in different patterns. The common thread in Project IV is that all these paradoxes have the notion of self-reference in common.

Project V

Study the "proof" below that all angles in figure 1 are right angles, and find the fallacy in it.

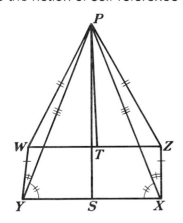

Fig. 1

Proof. The base angle *WYS* in figure 1 represents an arbitrary angle; the base angle *SXZ* is a right angle. All we need to show is that angle *WYS* equals angle *ZXS*, and to do this it suffices to show that angle *WYP* equals angle *ZXP* and angle *PYS* equals angle *PXS*. To begin, let angles *WYS* and *SXZ* be as shown, and let *S* be the midpoint of the line *YX*. Extend *YW* until it has the same length as *XZ*, and let *T* be the midpoint of *WZ*. Moreover, since *WZ* is not parallel to *YX*, the perpendicular bisectors of *WZ* and *YX* must meet at some point, say *P*. Evidently, *PW* and *PZ* are equal, since *P* is the perpendicular bisector of *WZ*; similarly, *PY* and *PX* have the same length. Now all that remains is putting together the right pieces: the three sides of triangle *YWP* are known to be equal, respectively, to the sides of triangle *ZXP*; thus these triangles are congruent and their corresponding angles *WYP* and *ZXP* are equal. The triangle *YPX* is isosceles, since *PY* equals *PX*; thus its base angles *PYS* and *PXS* are equal.

Guide: Your only guide here is the standard warning given to all mathematics students: although pictures may help you to "see" the answer to a problem, never rely too heavily on the exact form of your picture.

Project VI

One recent group of paradoxes comes from the use of "supermachines," which can perform any finite task in a finite amount of time. Using a supermachine, we can produce a wide variety of paradoxes. Just attach your supermachine to a light bulb and push a ball off a one-foot-high table. Use your machine to turn the light bulb on while the ball travels one-half the distance to the floor. Similarly, make the machine turn the bulb off as the ball travels half the remaining distance to the floor (to $1/2^2$ feet from the floor). Then make your machine turn the bulb on again as the ball travels halfway to the floor again (to $1/2^3$ feet from the floor). Repeating this process, your supermachine will turn the light bulb on and off an infinite number of times in less than one second—the time it takes the ball to reach the floor. Examine the question of whether the bulb is on or off when the ball hits the floor. As you can see, the question cannot be answered. Design five paradoxical tasks for your supermachine to perform.

Guide: In Reference 3 you will find a method for making your supermachine perform infinitely many tasks in an exactly specified amount of time. Supermachine paradoxes are true logical paradoxes.

For further study look in the references below.
At this point you think you are finished.
Let me remind you, I can never lie to you.
So believe me—there is one project yet to do.
Every effort should be made to find and do it.

REFERENCES

1. Bell, E. T. *Men of Mathematics.* New York: Simon & Schuster, 1937.
2. Bolzano, Bernard. *Paradoxes of the Infinite.* New Haven, Conn.: Yale University Press, 1950.
3. Casazza, Peter G. "Paradox Lost." *Alabama Journal of Mathematics* 1 (Spring 1977): 66–74.
4. DeMorgan, Augustus. *A Budget of Paradoxes.* New York: Dover Publications, 1954.
5. Dodgson, Charles Lutwidge. *The Complete Works of Lewis Carroll.* New York: Random House, 1939.
6. Fellow, Bragdon. *Diabolical Diversions.* New York: Doubleday & Co., 1980.
7. Fixx, James. *Games for the Super-Intelligent.* New York: Doubleday & Co., 1972.
8. Fixx, James. *More Games for the Super-Intelligent.* New York: Doubleday & Co., 1972.
9. Gardner, Martin. *The Unexpected Hanging and Other Mathematical Diversions.* New York: Simon & Schuster, 1968.
10. Gilbert, W. S. *The Savoy Operas.* London: Macmillan & Co., 1959.
11. Grunbaum, Adolf. *Modern Science and Zeno's Paradoxes.* Middletown, Conn.: Wesleyan University Press, 1963.
12. Hofstadter, Douglas R. *Gödel, Escher, Bach: An Eternal Golden Braid.* New York: Vintage Books, 1980.
13. Martin, Robert L. *The Paradox of the Liar.* New Haven, Conn.: Yale University Press, 1970.
14. Newman, James R. *The World of Mathematics.* 4 vols. New York: Simon & Schuster, 1956.
15. O'Beirne, T. H. *Puzzles and Paradoxes.* New York: Oxford University Press, 1956.
16. *Oxford English Dictionary.* 1981 ed., s.v. "paradox."
17. Quine, W. V. *Theories and Things.* Cambridge, Mass.: Harvard University Press, 1981.
18. Russell, Bertrand. *The Principles of Mathematics.* Cambridge, England: W. W. Norton & Co., 1902.
19. Cervantes Saavedra, Miguel de. *Don Quixote.* Translated by Walter Sarkie. New York: New American Library, Signet Classic, 1964.
20. Smullyan, Raymond. *What Is the Name of This Book?* Englewood Cliffs, N.J.: Prentice-Hall, 1978.
21. Smullyan, Raymond. *This Book Needs No Title.* Englewood Cliffs, N.J.: Prentice-Hall, 1980.
22. Sterne, Laurence. *Tristram Shandy.* New York: Carolton House, 1925.
23. *The Encyclopedia of Philosophy,* vol. 8, s.v. "Zeno," by Gregory Vlasto. New York: Macmillan and The Free Press, 1967.
24. Vlasto, Gregory. "Zeno's Race Course." *Journal of the History of Philosophy* 4 (2) (1966): 95–108.
25. Weaver, Warren. "Lewis Carroll: Mathematician." *Scientific American,* April 1956.

Teacher Notes

Project I

According to the *Oxford English Dictionary,* the word *paradox* comes from the Greek *paradoxus,* meaning "contrary to received opinion or expectation." The earliest reference to the word in the dictionary is 1540. Some of the common uses of the word are (1) a statement or tenet contrary to received opinion or belief; (2) a conclusion contrary to what the audience has been led up to; (3) a statement that, on the face of it, seems self-contradictory but may actually be well founded; (4) a statement that is actually self-contradictory.

Project II

1. Who shaves the barber? If he shaves himself, this contradicts the statement that the barber only shaves those who do not shave themselves. If he does not shave himself, this contradicts the statement that the barber shaves all those people who do not shave themselves. (Some of your students may note that if the barber is a woman no paradox exists!)

2. Is the statement in this box true or false? If it is a true statement, then it is true that "the statement in this box is false," so it is also a false statement. If it is a false statement, then "the statement in this box is (*not*) false," and hence it must be true.

3. If statement 3 is true, then two of the statements in the box must be false (and 3 is true), so that both 1 and 2 are false. But 1 is true. If statement 3 is false, then there are *not* two false statements in the box. But now statements 2 and 3 are false and statement 1 is true.

4. Part of the statement saying you should *never* exaggerate is itself an exaggeration.

5. This statement *is* a generality. So by the same argument as in example 2, it is a paradox.

6. This is not a paradox in the true sense. It is merely something that defies our intuition. The conflict occurs because of the phrase "could have written his entire autobiography." The reference is in past tense and leaves the impression that the autobiography could have been completed at some earlier time, whereas Shandy would actually need to write "forever." This looks less paradoxical if you change the phrase to read "could be writing his entire autobiography."

Project III

1. Don Quixote tells of a visit to a strange land with a curious custom. Every visitor there is asked, "Why did you come here?" If the visitor answers truthfully, all is well. But one who lies is hanged. One day a stranger answered this question by saying, "I came to be hanged." This created a paradox. For if they hang him, then his answer was truthful and they should have set him free. But if they do not hang him, then he lied and so they should have hanged him.

2. The Unexpected Hanging paradox goes as follows: A man has been sentenced to hang, with the following stipulations: He must be hanged within seven days, he must be hanged exactly at noon, and the day on which he is to be hanged must be a complete surprise to him. Having nothing to do in his cell, he tries to figure out when he will be hanged. He quickly realizes that they cannot hang him on the seventh day, for if they haven't hanged him by noon of the sixth day, then there is only one possible day left to do it, the seventh day, and he would know it, so it wouldn't be a surprise. But then they can't hang him on the sixth day, since if they haven't hanged him by noon of the fifth day (and he already knows they cannot hang him on the seventh day) it must be the sixth day, and therefore it isn't a surprise. Continuing this argument, he decides they cannot hang him on any day except the first and have it be a surprise; hence it cannot be a surprise at all, because he knows they must hang him on the first day. It appears that this is a true logical paradox, despite many attempts to find a fallacy in the argument. The paradox hinges on the not completely well-defined word *surprise.* Interestingly enough, the paradox disappears if we merely add to the stipulations the phrase, "or they may not hang him at all." That is, by putting in the alternative that they may not hang him at all, they can now hang him on any day (even the last) and have it be a "surprise."

3. The exact quote from Paul's letter to Titus is:

> One of themselves, even a prophet of their own,
> said, The Cretans are always liars . . .

This paradox can be explained if we assume this statement is a lie and some Cretans do tell the truth.

4. In this wonderful fable, Achilles tries to explain to the Tortoise a two-step argument followed by a conclusion from Euclid:

A. **(Argument 1):** Things that are equal to the same are equal to each other.

B. **(Argument 2):** The two sides of this triangle are things that are equal to the same.

Z. **(Conclusion):** The two sides of this triangle are equal to each other.

Achilles explains that you must accept A and B as true and conclude that Z is true. But the Tortoise cannot accept the conclusion. So they agree to make the "conclusion" an "assumption" and call it (C): If A and B are true, then Z must be true. But now the Tortoise still cannot accept Z as true and introduces (D): If A, B, and C are true, then Z must be true. Since the Tortoise still cannot accept Z as true, they state (E): If A, B, C, and D are true, then Z must be true. Luckily at this point, the narrator goes to the bank and we do not hear the end of the argument. This "paradox" is one of *infinite regression*. Lewis Carroll has set up a situation where each assumption requires a new assumption, so the process goes on "forever" and we never get to the conclusion.

5. Zeno's paradoxes on motion can be stated in many ways. One version is given below.

A. The Dichotomy: If a runner is to traverse a unit interval, she must first travel half the interval in half the time, and, by the same argument, by traversing the first half, she must traverse the first one-quarter in one-quarter of the time. Continuing, the runner must traverse an infinite regression of subintervals of lengths

$$\cdots, \ \frac{1}{2^n}, \ \cdots, \frac{1}{2^3}, \ \frac{1}{2^2}, \ \frac{1}{2}.$$

To accomplish this, the runner would have had to be running for a past eternity and hence could not have started to run a finite time ago.

B. Achilles and the Tortoise: If Achilles runs tens times faster than a Tortoise and starts only 1000 yards behind, he can never overtake the Tortoise. For when Achilles has traveled the 1000 yards to where the Tortoise began, the Tortoise is now 100 yards in front of him. When Achilles travels this 100 yards, the Tortoise has traveled 10 more yards and so is that far in front of him. When Achilles travels this 10 yards, the Tortoise moves 1 more yard in front of him. Thus, Achilles can get closer and closer to the Tortoise but can never overtake him. Each time Achilles reaches the point where the Tortoise was, the Tortoise has moved a little distance ahead.

C. The Arrow Paradox: At any given instant, an arrow in flight is not moving (since it cannot move "within" that instant of time). But there is no time between "instants," and so the arrow is not moving there either. That is, the arrow is not moving at all.

D. The Paradox of the Stadium: We have rows of points A and B surrounding a fixed stadium S. (See fig. 2.) We have row A move to the left at the rate of 1 point per instant and row B move to the right at this same rate. (See fig. 3.) But this is impossible because at some intervening time B1 must have been directly below A2 and there *is no* intervening time in an "instant."

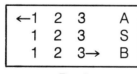

Fig. 2   Fig. 3

At this point, the student is "in a paradox." He or she has done numbers 1–5 and discovered they are all paradoxes. If one of these six exercises is not a paradox, it must be number 6. But now it isn't a surprise as I promised it would be—and I never lie. However, if number 6 is a paradox, then I lied in saying only five of them were paradoxes. Realizing he or she is in a paradox, the student should decide not to conclude anything about number 6 (and hence be "surprised" that it is not a paradox).

6. The quote of Gilbert is
How quaint the ways of paradox;
at common sense she clearly mocks.

Project IV

1. A. How about the encyclopedia that lists all those encyclopedias, and only those encyclopedias, that do not list themselves?

   B. Or the taxi driver who drives all those people to work, and only those people, who do not drive themselves?

2.

The statement in Box A is false.

Box A

1. At least one statement in this box is false. 2. 2 + 2 = 4

3. A. Never say never.

   B. I always lie.

4. A. The bumper sticker that says:
   "Eliminate Bumper Stickers."

   B. Sign on wall:
   "Down with graffitti."

Project V

The fallacy in this "proof" is that the line from P to Y will actually pass to the left of the point W; WYP and PYS do add up to a right angle, but their sum is not WYS. Given the incorrect picture above, everything stated in the "proof" is correct; only the conclusion is false. This should teach students not to rely too heavily on "pictures."

Project VI

Have your supermachine paint your house red while the light is on and paint it green while the light is off; or open a door while the light is on and close it while the light is off; or wash the dog while the light is on and dry it off while the light is off; or write a sentence and erase it; or go to the moon and come back, and so on.

The final "acrostic" is their last hint that this entire project was written as an acrostic. If they take the first letter from each *sentence* (without those included in parentheses or in boxes or the P's in the "Projects"), it will spell out:
PROJECT NUMBER VII: TELL WHY THE FOLLOWING IS A PARADOX:
THE NEXT SENTENCE YOU READ
   WILL BE TRUE.
THE LAST STATEMENT YOU
   JUST READ IS FALSE.

Continued Fractions

JOHN A. DOSSEY

THE term *continued fraction* refers to mathematical objects such as those shown below. These "fractions" result from a wide variety of circumstances and find applications in almost as wide an area of theoretical and practical settings. This unit is designed to assist you in the study of the development of continued fractions, their basic theory, and some of their applications in areas outside of mathematics.

$$x = 1 + \cfrac{1}{2 + \cfrac{1}{3 + \cfrac{1}{4 + \cfrac{1}{5}}}} \qquad\qquad y = 1 + \cfrac{1}{2 + \cfrac{1}{2 + \cfrac{1}{2 + \cfrac{1}{2 + \cdots}}}}$$

The two continued fractions illustrated above are known as *simple continued fractions* because all the "numerators" involved are 1's. We shall consider only simple continued fractions in this guide; if you are interested in more general classes of continued fractions, you might consult Reference 2 (vol. 2, chap. 34). You may also wish to consult other texts in the reference list to amplify the materials presented in this unit or to extend your understanding of the concepts and skills through additional reading and practice.

In order to complete the activities in this unit, you should have studied the material that is normally contained in the algebra taught in the first two years of college preparatory algebra. You should also have a general understanding of mathematical induction and the notion of the limit of a sequence. Other than these skills and concepts, you will need to perform only the basic whole number and rational number operations.

Projects

Project 1

Given a positive rational number, convert it to its simple continued fraction form.

Guide: The creation of the simple continued fraction expansion of a rational number is fairly easy to develop. As an example of this process, let us examine the development of the continued fraction expansion for the fraction 7/3. Our task is to write 7/3 in the continued fraction form where all the "numerators" in the chain of the expansion are 1's.

We begin by writing 7/3 as 2 + 1/3. At this point we have satisfied the requirements for the continued fraction expansion. However, we could continue the process and write the 1/3 as

$$\cfrac{1}{2 + \cfrac{1}{1}},$$

giving the number 7/3 the continued fraction expansion

$$7/3 = 2 + \cfrac{1}{2 + \cfrac{1}{1}}.$$

Either of these expansions is appropriate and correct for the continued fraction representation of 7/3. Mathematicians record these representations by writing them respectively as $\langle 2;3\rangle$ and $\langle 2;2,1\rangle$. Note the use of the semicolon to separate the whole number from the lead denominator in the chain of the continued fraction.

Using the same procedure, we can change 75/31 into a continued fraction through the following sequence of steps:

$$\frac{75}{31} = 2 + \frac{13}{31} = 2 + \cfrac{1}{\frac{31}{13}} = 2 + \cfrac{1}{2 + \frac{5}{13}} = 2 + \cfrac{1}{2 + \cfrac{1}{\frac{13}{5}}}$$

$$= 2 + \cfrac{1}{2 + \cfrac{1}{2 + \frac{3}{5}}} = 2 + \cfrac{1}{2 + \cfrac{1}{2 + \cfrac{1}{\frac{5}{3}}}} = 2 + \cfrac{1}{2 + \cfrac{1}{2 + \cfrac{1}{1 + \frac{2}{3}}}}$$

$$= 2 + \cfrac{1}{2 + \cfrac{1}{2 + \cfrac{1}{1 + \cfrac{1}{\frac{3}{2}}}}} = 2 + \cfrac{1}{2 + \cfrac{1}{2 + \cfrac{1}{1 + \cfrac{1}{1 + \frac{1}{2}}}}} = \langle 2;2,2,1,1,2 \rangle$$

We could have extended the process one more step and written the 1/2 as

$$1 + \cfrac{1}{1 + \frac{1}{1}}.$$

This would have given the expansion $\langle 2;2,2,1,1,1,1 \rangle$.

This process can be shortened through the use of repeated division as shown in the calculation in figure 1.

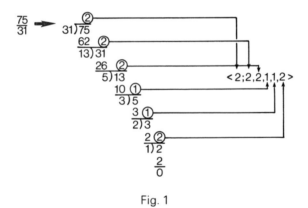

Fig. 1

Now that you have had some experience with simple continued fractions, we might define them a little more carefully. We might say that a simple continued fraction is a number of the form

$$a_1 + \cfrac{1}{a_2 + \cfrac{1}{a_3 + \cfrac{1}{a_4 + \cdots}}}$$

where a_1 is an integer and all of $a_2, a_3, a_4, \ldots$ are nonzero integers.

Practice converting rational numbers into continued fraction form. The exercises in References 9 and 12 will be of great aid in practicing this skill. Then write your continued fraction forms in both the long, chain form illustrated in the definition and in the more compact notation listing just the lead terms from the denominators in the continued fraction's expansion.

Project 2

Explain and justify some basic properties of the simple continued fraction of a rational number.

Guide: In your completion of the continued fraction expansions for the rational numbers you picked to work with in Project 1, what patterns did you note in the continued fraction expansions? Some of the basic patterns you should have noted are the following:

1. The continued fraction expansion for a given rational number always terminates. That is, the process eventually reaches a denominator of 1 if continued through enough stages.

2. Each rational number has a unique continued fraction expansion when the process is allowed to continue until a final denominator of 1 is reached.

3. The continued fraction expansions for the rational numbers p/q and q/p for p and q nonzero and $p < q$ are related by $p/q = \langle 0; a, b, c, \ldots, z \rangle$ and $q/p = \langle a; b, c, d, \ldots, z \rangle$.

4. If the continued fraction expansion for a given number terminates, than the given number is a rational number.

These four properties are important properties for the continued fraction expansion of a rational number. Properties 1 and 4 constitute a major theorem: *A continued fraction expansion of a number terminates if and only if the given number is a rational number.*

For assistance in studying these properties, consult the material presented in References 9 (pp. 4–6), 11 (pp. 188–89), and 12 (pp. 9–19).

Project 3

Given a continued fraction expansion for a real number, give the convergents for that continued fraction and an approximate decimal value for the number represented by the continued fraction.

Guide: In this section of the study of continued fractions, we enlarge our view of continued fractions by including nonterminating continued fractions. In addition, we shall change our orientation a bit, for we shall be starting with the continued fraction and working back to find, or approximate, the number it represents.

For example, consider the number given by the following continued fraction:

$$x = 3 + \cfrac{1}{7 + \cfrac{1}{15 + \cfrac{1}{1 + \cfrac{1}{292 + \cdots}}}}$$

We can drop off the terms in the expansion at any point and check to see what number is represented by the remaining portion by reversing the process we used to get the expansions. For example, we could terminate the fraction after the 7, and we would have $x = 3 + 1/7$, or $3.\overline{142857}$. If we terminated the fraction after the 15 we would have

$$x = 3 + \cfrac{1}{7 + \cfrac{1}{15}} = 3 + \cfrac{1}{\cfrac{106}{15}} = 3 + \cfrac{15}{106} = \cfrac{333}{106} \doteq 3.1415094.$$

As you might guess, further terminations lead to values that get closer and closer to the value for π. These fractions that result from successive termination of the continued fraction expansion for x (3/1, 22/7, 333/106, 355/113, 9208/2931, ...) are called the *convergents* for x. The first term in the continued fraction expansion, a_1, is called the first convergent; the result of the calculation of $a_1 + 1/a_2$ is called the second convergent; and so on as one continues to terminate the expansion after specified leading terms in its sequence of denominators.

If the first convergent, $a_1/1$, is represented by p_1/q_1, the second convergent, $a_1 + 1/a_2$, is represented by p_2/q_2, and so on, several interesting properties of the convergents can be developed. To understand these properties of the convergents, you must be able to quickly convert a given continued fraction back into its convergents by terminating its expansion and finding the value of the truncated expansion. Try this with several continued fractions. Look for patterns in the calculations as you find the exact or approximate values of the continued fractions. Several practice problems are contained in References 9 (pp. 8–9) and 12 (pp. 25–26). Use both terminating and nonterminating continued fractions in your work.

Project 4

The convergents for a continued fraction satisfy several important properties. Identify the basic relationships between the numerators and denominators of the convergents and explain why the patterns hold for the continued fraction expansions of rational numbers.

Guide: Consider the set of all convergents for a given rational number. These fractions represent the values obtained by truncating the continued fraction expansion for this rational number by stopping after each leading term in the sequence of denominators. This series of fractions p_1/q_1, p_2/q_2, p_3/q_3, ... continues until the last convergent is reached, p_n/q_n. Each successive value gets closer to the value of the rational number we started with until we reach it with the last convergent. The numerators, p_i, and the denominators, q_i, of these convergents have several interesting patterns in them. These patterns result in the following theorems:

1. The numerators p_i and the denominators q_i of the ith convergent of the continued fraction $\langle a_1; a_2, a_3, a_4, \ldots, a_n \rangle$ satisfy the equations

$$p_i = a_i p_{i-1} + p_{i-2}$$
$$q_i = a_i q_{i-1} + q_{i-2} \qquad (i = 3, 4, 5, \ldots, n)$$

with the initial values for p_i and q_i given by $p_1 = a_1$, $q_1 = 1$, $p_2 = a_1 a_2 + 1$, and $q_2 = a_2$.

2. If p_i and q_i are the numerator and denominator of the ith convergent to $\langle a_1; a_2, a_3, \ldots, a_n \rangle$ and $i > 1$, then we have $p_i q_{i-1} - p_{i-1} q_i = (-1)^i$.

3. The convergents for a continued fraction $\langle a_1; a_2, a_3, \ldots, a_n \rangle$ are always in lowest terms.

You should work out several examples of each of these relationships and see how the numerators and denominators of successive convergents are related to each other by theorems 1 and 2. In addition, you should study the proofs of these properties as given in References 5 (pp. 7–18) and 8 (pp. 19–28).

Project 5

Examine the properties of convergents when they are applied to infinite continued fractions. Which properties continue to hold and what additional patterns can be found? Explain and illustrate your findings.

Guide: The theory of infinite continued fractions closely parallels the theory of continued fractions that terminate. The big differences are in the type of number they represent. Since a continued fraction represents a real number and a continued fraction terminates if and only if it represents a rational number, we have the result that nonterminating continued fractions represent irrational numbers.

The properties expressed by (1) and (2) in the properties discussed for finite continued fractions in Project 4 extend immediately to infinite continued fractions. However, we obtain some new results for infinite continued fractions. Before we look at them, let us stop and generate the continued fraction for the irrational number $\sqrt{2}$. There are two ways we might approach this task.

The first approach is to examine the number. We know that the $\sqrt{2}$ is larger than 1 and less than 2. Thus, $\sqrt{2} = 1 + 1/x_2$. Solving this equation, we get $x_2 = \sqrt{2} + 1$. This gives us the start of an expansion,

$$\sqrt{2} = 1 + \cfrac{1}{\sqrt{2} + 1}.$$

But inspection reveals that the largest integer less than $\sqrt{2}+1$ is 2, so we can further advance the expansion for $\sqrt{2}$ by writing it as

$$\sqrt{2} = 1 + \cfrac{1}{2 + \cfrac{1}{x_3}},$$

where x_3 results from $x_2 = a_2 + 1/x_3$, or $x_2 = 2 + 1/x_3$. Solving this, we get

$$x_3 = \cfrac{1}{x_2 - 2}, \text{ or } \cfrac{1}{\sqrt{2}-1}.$$

Rationalizing, we get $x_3 = \sqrt{2} + 1$, and the largest integer less than x_3 is 2. This process continues, giving the expansion for $\sqrt{2}$ as

$$1 + \cfrac{1}{2 + \cfrac{1}{2 + \cfrac{1}{2 + \cfrac{1}{2 + \cdots}}}}$$

A second method to arrive at this result is to consider the equation $x^2 = 2$. We can write this as $x^2 - 2 = 0$, or $(x + 1)(x - 1) = 1$. Working with this last form, we can write $x - 1 = 1/(x + 1)$. Working with this, we further see that $x = 1 + 1/(1 + x)$. On replacing the x in the numerator of the continued fraction by the value $1 + 1/(1 + x)$, to which x is set equal, we get

$$x = 1 + \cfrac{1}{1 + 1 + \cfrac{1}{1 + x}}.$$

Continuing this process, we see that we can do this indefinitely, resulting in the expansion for x as

$$1 + \cfrac{1}{2 + \cfrac{1}{2 + \cfrac{1}{2 + \cfrac{1}{2 + \cdots}}}}$$

Since x is easily seen to be the square root of 2, we have a second method for extracting the infinite continued fraction expansion for $\sqrt{2}$.

Find the continued fraction expansions for several irrational numbers, such as $\sqrt{3}$, $\sqrt{5}$, and $\sqrt{7}$. Look at the expansions. Do you notice any patterns in the leading terms of the denominators in the expansions? You should, for all these numbers are irrational numbers resulting from quadratic equations. (Why?) Quadratic irrationals (which is what we call these kinds of numbers) have continued fractions that result in infinite expansions with periodic patterns in the leading terms of their denominators. For instance, $\sqrt{6} = \langle 2; 2,4,2,4,2,4,2,4,\ldots \rangle = \langle 2; \overline{2,4} \rangle$, and $\sqrt{43} = \langle 6; \overline{1,1,3,1,5,1,3,1,1,12} \rangle$. Calculate several of the continued fraction expansions for quadratic irrational numbers. Can you find any other patterns in the leading terms of their denominators?

Additional information on quadratic irrationals and their continued fraction expansions, as well as on infinite continued expansions, can be found in References 9 (pp. 38–53) and 12 (pp. 51–61).

Project 6

Given an infinite continued fraction, use the properties of infinite continued fractions and their convergents, along with the limit concept, to approximate the value of an infinite continued fraction within a given interval.

Guide: Look back to the convergents you calculated in working with the properties of the convergents (Project 4). Did you notice any patterns in the way in which the convergents approached the actual value of the continued fraction? You should have. If not, look again, this time graphing the convergents on a number line as they relate to the actual value of the continued fraction.

You should have noted that the convergents are alternately greater than and less than the value of the continued fraction as they approached that value. Moreover, each successive convergent falls between the two that preceded it. Establish this result for terminating continued fractions. For assistance, you may wish to consult Reference 4 (pp. 85–88).

Repeat this same process, examining the relationship of convergents to the value of an infinite continued fraction. Does the same pattern hold? Try to establish a proof of it if it does. For some assistance in completing this project, see Reference 12 (pp. 61–70). What does all this have to do with the notion of a limit of a sequence?

Project 7

Develop a report detailing an application of continued fractions. The report should carefully state the problem, describe the application of continued fractions to solve it, and show that the results fit the requirements of the original problem.

Guide: There are several applications of continued fractions in both mathematics and areas outside of mathematics. Within mathematics, the applications of continued fractions have been closely tied to establishing rational approximations to irrational numbers. For instance, what rational numbers serve as good approximations to π, to e, or to $\sqrt{n}$ (where n is not a perfect square)? To report on these applications, you may wish to consult the information found in References 2 (vol. 2, chap. 32, articles 12–16), 9 (pp. 34–37), and 12 (pp. 70–76). What is Hurwitz's theorem and what does it have to do with approximations involving continued fractions?

Another application of continued fractions arises in the area of mechanical engineering. Here, the problem is the design of a gearbox that will take a given input of x revolutions per minute and deliver an output of y revolutions per minute. This can be related to the previous application when one considers that when the input is scaled to 1, the output is scaled to the value of y/x. Unfortunately, mechanical engineers are constrained to work with gears having from 20 to 100 teeth on them. The value of y/x may require them to search for a sequence of gears within this range and then to pick the set of gears (thus a rational approximation) that delivers the value closest to y/x. Ample information on this problem can be found in References 9 (pp. 31–34) and 1 (see pp. 204–16 for a full account of continued fractions and gearbox designs).

A third area of applications of continued fractions comes from the area of botany. For years, botanists have tried to understand the recurring appearance of the sequence 1, 1, 2, 3, 5, 8, 13, 21, 34, 65, … in many natural settings. This sequence, known as the Fibonacci sequence, is found, for instance, in the counts of the patterns of seeds on a sunflower, leaves on a tree, or "eyes" on the side of a pineapple. An interesting explanation for such patterns is given in Reference 8. Additional information on the topic can be found in Reference 3. To understand it fully, you will want to look at the geometric interpretation of convergents as outlined in Reference 12 (pp. 77–79). The word *phyllotaxis* in Coxeter's title (Reference 3) refers to the arrangement of leaves on plants.

Another series of applications dealing with the calendar and the prediction of eclipses appears in Reference 2 (in vol. 2, chap. 32, in the examples at the end of article 16, and in the footnotes appended to the text at that point).

A final area in which applications of continued fractions appear is discussed in Reference 13 (chap. 3), in which the role that approximations play in designing musical instruments is illustrated. The chapter entitled "The Well-Tempered Clavichord" examines the number of notes in a scale that is pleasing (harmonious) to our ears. If you are interested in music, you may find this application quite interesting.

Project 8

Write a report on the history of continued fractions, listing the important breakthroughs and the individuals associated with them. Arrange your report in a chronological manner showing how each new discovery has furthered our knowledge of continued fractions.

Guide: To find information on the history of continued fractions, you may wish to consult References 2, 9, and 12. In addition, you will probably want to look at the other references.

REFERENCES

1. Christman, John M. *Shop Mathematics*. New York: Macmillan Co., 1922.

*2. Chrystal, G. *Algebra: An Elementary Textbook*. 2 vols. 1889. Reprint. New York: Chelsea Publishing Co., 1964. (See especially chaps. 32, 33, and 34 of vol. 2.)

3. Coxeter, H. S. MacDonald. "The Role of Intermediate Convergents in Tait's Explanation for Phyllotaxis." *Journal of Algebra* 20 (1972):167–75.

*4. Davenport, Harold. *The Higher Arithmetic*. New York: Harper & Row, 1960.

5. Dickson, Leonard Eugene. *History of the Theory of Numbers*. 3 vols. New York: Chelsea Publishing Co., 1950.

6. Eves, Howard. *An Introduction to the History of Mathematics*. 4th ed. New York: Holt, Rinehart & Winston, 1976.

*7. Hardy, G. H., and E. M. Wright. *An Introduction to the Theory of Numbers*. London: Oxford University Press, 1965.

8. Jean, Roger V. *The Use of Continued Fractions in Botany*. UMAP Module Unit 571. Newton, Mass.: Education Development Center, 1981.

9. Moore, Charles G. *An Introduction to Continued Fractions*. Washington, D.C.: National Council of Teachers of Mathematics, 1964.

*10. Niven, Ivan. *Irrational Numbers*. Washington, D.C.: Mathematical Association of America, 1956.

*11. Niven, Ivan, and H. S. Zuckerman. *An Introduction to the Theory of Numbers*. 4th ed. New York: John Wiley & Sons, 1980.

12. Olds, C. D. *Continued Fractions*. Washington, D.C.: Mathematical Association of America, 1963. (Originally published as an SMSG Monograph.)

13. Penny, David E. *Perspectives in Mathematics*, chap. 3. Menlo Park, Calif.: W. A. Benjamin, 1972.

14. Smith, David Eugene. *History of Mathematics*. 2 vols. New York: Dover Publications, 1958.

---

*Denotes an advanced textbook requiring some mathematical maturity.

Teacher Notes

This unit on continued fractions requires the student to complete a rather difficult series of projects. The first two projects involve the student in looking at the writing of continued fractions and the conversion of terminating continued fractions into rational numbers. In the next group, the student must master the basic theoretical relationships holding for terminating and nonterminating continued fractions. This set of requirements can be eased for average students by having them understand the requirements but not prove them. Advanced students should prove the results. The final two projects examine the application and history of continued fractions.

In the following materials, the main objective of each section will be discussed, as will sample problems and additional references. The sample problems might be given to the students to measure their degree of mastery of the requirements.

References 9 and 12 each contain the bulk of materials needed in the unit. Reference 9 is available from the National Council of Teachers of Mathematics, 1906 Association Drive, Reston, VA 22091. Reference 12 is available from the Mathematical Association of America, 1529 Eighteenth Street, NW, Washington, DC 20036. Reference 8 can be obtained from the Education Development Center, 55 Chapel Street, Newton, MA 02160. The other references should be available in a nearby major college or university library.

Project 1

To complete this project, the student should develop the ability to rapidly shift rational numbers from fraction form to continued fraction form. In doing so, the student should have the opportunity to compare the continued fraction forms for a/b and b/a, for a pair of fractions a/b and c/d where $a/b < c/d$, and, for advanced students, where the rational number is negative. Some examples of rational numbers and their continued fraction expansions that are worth examining follow.

$$3/7 = \langle 0;2,3 \rangle \text{ or } \langle 0;2,2,1 \rangle \qquad 167/81 = \langle 2;16,5 \rangle \text{ or } \langle 2;16,4,1 \rangle$$
$$7/3 = \langle 2;3 \rangle \text{ or } \langle 2;2,1 \rangle \qquad 4/7 = \langle 0;1,1,3 \rangle \text{ or } \langle 0;1,1,2,1 \rangle$$
$$7 = \langle 7; \rangle \qquad 23/100 = \langle 0;4,2,1,7 \rangle \text{ or } \langle 0;4,2,1,6,1 \rangle$$
$$1/7 = \langle 0;7 \rangle \text{ or } \langle 0;6,1 \rangle \qquad 251/802 = \langle 0;3,5,8,6 \rangle \text{ or } \langle 0;3,5,8,5,1 \rangle$$

Note: 1. If the continued fraction does not terminate with a 1, it can have its last term decreased by 1 and an additional term of 1 added to it.

2. The relationship between the expansions for a/b and b/a where $a/b < b/a$ is given by $\langle 0;\alpha,\beta,\dots,\omega \rangle < \langle \alpha;\beta,\dots,\omega \rangle$.

Project 2

The necessary background for these properties can be found in References 2, 9, or 12. The proofs are presented in the best form and with the most detail in Reference 12. Properties 1 and 4 are probably best treated as separate properties first rather than being combined into an if-and-only-if form. The necessary and sufficient conditions for termination should be discussed with the student, however.

Project 3

This project brings the student back to manipulations involving the partial quotients in the continued fraction's expansion. The student should have the opportunity to examine both terminating and infinite continued fractions at this point, but not much emphasis should be put on the nature of the infinite continued fraction.

Some potential practice problems follow:

$$\langle 0;3,5,8,6 \rangle = 251/802 \text{ with convergents } 0,\ 1/3,\ 5/16,\ 41/131,\text{ and } 251/802$$
$$\langle 2;6,1,1,11,2 \rangle = 323/150 \text{ with convergents (first 5) } 2,\ 13/6,\ 15/7,\ 28/13,\text{ and } 323/150$$
$$\langle 0;3,3,3,3,3,3,3 \rangle = 1189/3927 \text{ with convergents (first 5) } 0,\ 1/3,\ 3/10,\ 10/33,\text{ and } 33/109$$
$$\langle 0;1,1,1,1,1,3,1,2,\dots \rangle \doteq 0.62138 \text{ with convergents (first 5) } 0,\ 1,\ 1/2,\ 2/3,\text{ and } 3/5$$

For a mastery of Project 3, the students should be able to work these and similar problems with ease.

Project 4

The properties that the convergents, and the numerators and denominators of the convergents, satisfy are well described in both Reference 9 and 12. One nice extension of the requirements that could be given to students is the methods for calculating successive convergents using the rectangular matrix form described in Reference 9. This calculational form is handy in dealing with the applications of continued fractions to gearbox design given later in the unit.

Project 5

The comments for this section are similar to those given for the preceding section. In particular, one might wish to examine the proofs and the differences in the proof structure for the properties as they relate to terminating continued fractions and as they relate to infinite continued fractions.

One nice side excursion at this point is to examine the relation between infinite continued fractions and Fibonacci numbers and the Fibonacci missing region puzzle. A good explanation of this material is given in Reference 12 (pp. 81–84). Additional material on Fibonacci numbers can be found in chapters 8 through 10 of *The Golden Section and Related Curiosa*, by Garth Runion (paperback, Scott Foresman, 1972).

Project 6

The study of the material for this project will call for careful work and the construction of some number line graphs. The problems are perhaps best approached by working through rational number expansions first and then going on to the infinite continued fractions. For each problem, the student should examine the order in which the convergents appear and the pattern—alternating—in which they surround the value of the number represented by the expansion.

Some attention should be paid to getting a solution to the value of an infinite continued fraction within 0.1 of the true value, within 0.01 of the true value, and so on. This can be done by finding the difference between the successive convergents. Since we know that the actual value resides between successive convergents, the process can stop when that distance gets less than the tolerance called for. Several problems of this type are called for in References 2 and 9.

Some discussion of Hurwitz's theorem would also be appropriate: *Given any irrational number ξ, there exist infinitely many rational numbers p/q such that*

$$\left| \xi - \frac{p}{q} \right| < \frac{1}{\sqrt{5}\, q^2}.$$

This in effect states that the convergents from some point on to the irrational number ξ are all within a small distance of the number and that distance is a function of the denominator q of the convergent.

Project 7

This is the portion of the unit that has the biggest payoff for the student. All the work up to this point has been selected so that the student could tackle one or more of these problems. The student guide, along with the references mentioned in it, gives the best sources for the work. All of them give worked-out examples and ample additional work for the student. The gearbox application and the botany examples are probably the most interesting to students at the secondary level.

Project 8

The material for this project is outlined in the student guide. The most helpful sources are probably References 9, 12, and 14. Additional information is given in Reference 2 in the footnotes to the chapters on continued fractions. Reference 5 gives additional references, but the text is a little difficult for secondary students to use.

Finding Equations from Tables of Values

D. P. JIM PREKEGES

TODAY we often look for mathematical models that approximately fit a particular situation or a particular set of data. In an algebra course, this model is usually an equation of the form

$$y = ax^r + bx^{r-1} + cx^{r-2} + ... + sx + t.$$

You have worked with equations of this form before—for example, when $r = 1$, the equation is $y = ax + b$, and when $r = 2$, the equation is $y = ax^2 + bx + c$.

We can ask the question, "Given the following data, how are x and y related?

x	0	1	2	3	4	5	6	7	8	9	10
y	3	5	11	21	35	53	75	101	131	165	203

We hope that relationship will be a polynomial function. In an attempt to find the relationship, we can guess, but we do not know whether it is linear, quadratic, or a higher-degree equation. We also do not know the value of the constant term. If we can answer questions such as these, then we can find the relationship.

There are mathematical techniques that can assist us in answering such questions. One of these techniques, known as a difference table, uses the ideas of finite differences.

Projects

Project 1

For each of the following, make a table of values using eight values for x, and then evaluate the difference table for each set of data:

1. $y = 3x + 5$
2. $y = 4x^2 + 3$
3. $y = 2x - 2$
4. $y = 3x^2 + 2x - 4$
5. $y = 4x^3$
6. $y = 2x^3 + 7x + 3$
7. $y = 3x^4$

Guide: To make a difference table, we first make a table of x values, and then find the y values. Next we take the differences of successive y values. We then take the differences of successive differences until the differences are the same. For example, for $y = 2x^2 + 3$, the tables of values and differences is shown in figure 1. Note that there are two lines in our difference table, that is, it took two lines of finding differences until all the differences were the same, 4 in our example. Note further that the values chosen for x differ by 1 as they increase. It is necessary when developing a difference table for the differences between the x values to be constant as x increases.

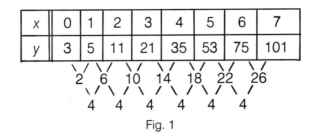

Fig. 1

Project 2

Make a chart showing the following data from Project 1.

Equation	Degree of equation	Number of lines in difference table
1		
2		
3		
4		
5		
6		
7		

Examine the data in the chart and determine a relationship between the *number of lines in the difference table* and the *degree of the equation.*

Project 3

Using your conclusions from Project 2, determine the degree of the equation that relates each *x* to the given *y* in the following:

1.

x	0	1	2	3	4	5	6	7	8
y	−7	−5	1	11	25	43	65	91	121

2.

x	0	1	2	3	4	5	6	7	8
y	3	4	17	54	127	248	429	682	1019

3.

x	0	1	2	3	4	5	6	7	8
y	−7	−2	3	8	13	18	23	28	33

4.

x	0	1	2	3	4	5	6	7	8
y	0	−1	2	9	20	35	54	77	104

5.

x	0	1	2	3	4	5	6	7	8
y	−1	−1	9	65	225	579	1229	2309	3975

6.

x	0	2	4	6	8	10	12
y	−2	8	26	52	86	128	178

(Notice the *x*'s are two apart, a constant difference.)

7.

x	0	1	2	3	4	5	6	7	8
y	5	6	13	32	69	130	221	348	517

Project Project 4

Determine the *x* and *y* relationship for each table of values from Project 3.

NCTM Projects to Enrich School Mathematics: Level 3

Guide: Study the difference table in figure 2 to determine the degree of the equation.

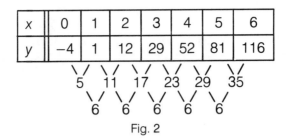

Fig. 2

Since the second line is constant (6), we know the equation is a second-degree equation, which has a general form of

$$y = ax^2 + bx + c.$$

Our goal is to find a, b, and c. From the table of values, we know that when $x = 2$, $y = 12$. Substituting this information into the general form, we get

$$12 = 4a + 2b + c.$$

Since this is an equation in three unknowns (a, b, c), we need three such equations to find the values of a, b, and c. When $x = 3$, then $y = 29$, and they are substituted into the general form to get

$$29 = 9a + 3b + c.$$

When $x = 4$, $y = 52$, and they're substituted into the general form to get

$$52 = 16a + 4b + c.$$

Now we have a system of three equations in three unknowns:

$$12 = 4a + 2b + c$$
$$29 = 9a + 3b + c$$
$$52 = 16a + 4b + c$$

Solving this system gives $a = 3$, $b = 2$, and $c = -4$. Using these values in the general form $y = ax^2 + bx + c$, we get

$$y = 3x^2 + 2x - 4,$$

the relationship between x and y for the given table of values.

Project 5

Figurate numbers are related to geometric figures. There are triangular numbers, square numbers, pentagonal numbers, hexagonal numbers, and so on. List the figurate numbers as they relate to three-sided regular figures (triangular numbers), four-sided regular figures (square numbers), . . . , and ten-sided regular figures. List the first six numbers for each type of figure. Put these numbers in the tabular form that follows. You will have to find patterns going across and down to complete the table. (The nth number and m sides will be completed later.)

# of sides	1st	2d	3d	4th	5th	6th ...nth
3						
4						
5						
6						
7						
8						
9						
10						
.						
.						
.						
m						

Guide: References 2 and 3 should assist you.

Project 6

Establish an equation for the *n*th term of the figurate numbers 3-sided through 10-sided. Apply your knowledge related to—

1. difference tables;
2. making systems of equations;
3. solving these systems.

Then develop an algebraic expression for the *n*th term in terms of *n*.

Guide: As an example for the 7-sided figurate numbers, Project 5 gives:

1st	2d	3d	4th	5th	6th ... *n*th
1	7	18	34	55	81

This leads us to the table in figure 3.

n	1	2	3	4	5	6
y	1	7	18	34	55	81

Fig. 3

Using the methods of Project 4, we find that the resulting equation is

$$y = \frac{5}{2}n^2 - \frac{3}{2}n,$$

or

$$y = \frac{n(5n - 3)}{2}.$$

Therefore, the *n*th term in terms of *n* is

$$\frac{n(5n - 3)}{2}.$$

Finding a pattern of *n*th terms could save you some work as the number of sides increases.

Now complete the last column of the table from Project 5, or the *n*th terms of the 3- through 10-sided figurate numbers.

Project 7

Complete the row for *m*-sided figurate numbers. Use the same ideas as in Project 6.

Guide: The following work demonstrates the procedure for the column of 4th figurate numbers. First make a table of values and then a difference table (see fig. 4).

# of sides	3	4	5	6	7	8	9	10
4th numbers	10	16	22	28	34	40	46	52

Fig. 4

Since the differences are constant, it is first-degree equation. By using methods of Project 4, the 4th figurate number for an *m*-sided figure is $6m - 8$.

Now complete the last row of the table from Project 5, or the 1st through 6th figurate numbers for an *m*-sided figure.

Project 8

Examine the pattern that exists in the column of *n*th figurate numbers, then give the algebraic expression for the *n*th figurate number that comes from the *m*-sided regular figure.

Project 9

Verify your result from Project 8 by extending your results of Project 7 to the *n*th figurate number. One way is to make a table of values and a difference table, then establish a system of equations and solve the system. (You will have to treat *m* as a constant, not a variable.)

REFERENCES

1. Your second-year high school algebra text.
2. Hughes, Barnabas. *Thinking through Problems*. Palo Alto, Calif.: Creative Publications, 1977.
3. National Council of Teachers of Mathematics. *Historical Topics for the Mathematics Classroom*. Thirty-first Yearbook. Washington, D.C.: The Council, 1969.

Teacher Notes

Project 1

The tables of values and the difference tables for each table of values are as follows:

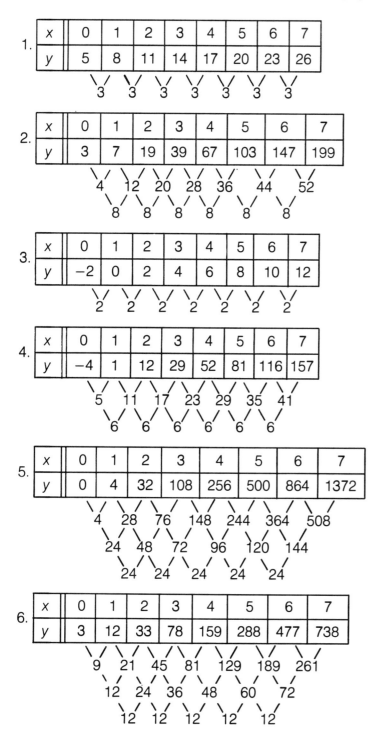

1.

x	0	1	2	3	4	5	6	7
y	5	8	11	14	17	20	23	26

3 3 3 3 3 3 3

2.

x	0	1	2	3	4	5	6	7
y	3	7	19	39	67	103	147	199

4 12 20 28 36 44 52

8 8 8 8 8 8

3.

x	0	1	2	3	4	5	6	7
y	−2	0	2	4	6	8	10	12

2 2 2 2 2 2 2

4.

x	0	1	2	3	4	5	6	7
y	−4	1	12	29	52	81	116	157

5 11 17 23 29 35 41

6 6 6 6 6 6

5.

x	0	1	2	3	4	5	6	7
y	0	4	32	108	256	500	864	1372

4 28 76 148 244 364 508

24 48 72 96 120 144

24 24 24 24 24

6.

x	0	1	2	3	4	5	6	7
y	3	12	33	78	159	288	477	738

9 21 45 81 129 189 261

12 24 36 48 60 72

12 12 12 12 12

7.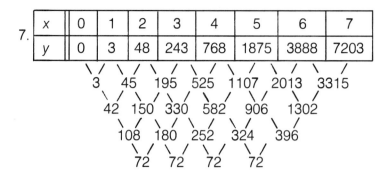

Project 2

The chart will be as follows:

Equation	Degree of equation	Number of lines in difference table
1	1	1
2	2	2
3	1	1
4	2	2
5	3	3
6	3	3
7	4	4

The desired relationship is that the <u>number of lines in the difference table</u> is the same as the <u>degree of the equation.</u>

Project 3

The students should realize they must find the number of lines in the difference table to determine the degree of the equation for each table of values.

Equation	Degree of equation
1	2
2	3
3	1
4	2
5	4
6	2
7	3

Project 4

The example shows how to put all the ideas above together and get the algebraic equation that shows how x relates to y. The equations are as follows:

	Table of Values		Equation

Table of Values	Equation
1	$y = 2x^2 - 7$
2	$y = 2x^3 - x + 3$
3	$y = 5x - 7$
4	$y = 2x^2 - 3x$
5	$y = x^4 - 2x^2 + x - 1$
6	$y = x^2 + 3x - 2$
7	$y = x^3 + 5$

Project 5

Figurate numbers exist in different parts of mathematics. The triangular numbers can be found in Pascal's triangle, and the square numbers have been used by your students many times. The table will look like the following:

# of sides	1st	2d	3d	4th	5th	6th . . . nth
3	1	3	6	10	15	21
4	1	4	9	16	25	36
5	1	5	12	22	35	51
6	1	6	15	28	45	66
7	1	7	18	34	55	81
8	1	8	21	40	65	96
9	1	9	24	46	75	111
10	1	10	27	52	85	126
.						
.						
.						
m						

Project 6

The example shows how to use all the previous ideas to find the nth figurate number for the 7-sided regular figure. The nth column will look like the following:

# of sides	nth
3	$\dfrac{n(n+1)}{2}$
4	n^2
5	$\dfrac{n(3n-1)}{2}$
6	$\dfrac{n(4n-2)}{2}$
7	$\dfrac{n(5n-3)}{2}$
8	$\dfrac{n(6n-4)}{2}$
9	$\dfrac{n(7n-5)}{2}$
10	$\dfrac{n(8n-6)}{2}$

If the student had written n^2 as $\dfrac{n(2n)}{2}$ and then $\dfrac{n(2n-0)}{2}$, he or she would have recognized the pattern and saved a great amount of work for the last few.

Project 7

The example again demonstrates the use of the ideas above to get a particular number in terms of m. The row for the figurate number with m sides will be as follows:

$$1 \qquad m \qquad 3m-3 \qquad 6m-8 \qquad 10m-15 \qquad 15m-24$$

Project 8

By looking at the set of nth numbers, the student should recognize by pattern that for the m-sided figurate numbers the nth number will **be**

$$\frac{n[(m-2)n-(m-4)]}{2}.$$

The student should notice that each nth number has the form $\dfrac{n(rn-p)}{2}$ where the r and p change; further, that r is two less than the number of sides and p is four less.

Project 9

Establish a table of values and a difference table:

x	1st	2d	3d	4th	5th	6th
y	1	m	$3m-3$	$6m-8$	$10m-15$	$15m-24$

$$\begin{array}{ccccccccc}
& m-1 & & 2m-3 & & 3m-5 & & 4m-7 & & 5m-9 \\
& & m-2 & & m-2 & & m-2 & & m-2 &
\end{array}$$

Hence, the relationship is a quadratic equation of the form

$$y = ax^2 + bx + c.$$

We now establish a system of three equations in three unknowns.

$$3m - 3 = 9a + 3b + c$$
$$6m - 8 = 16a + 4b + c$$
$$10m - 15 = 25a + 5b + c$$

Treating m as a constant and solving for a, b, and c, we get

$$a = \frac{m - 2}{2}, \quad b = \frac{-m + 4}{2}, \quad c = 0$$

and our relationship is

$$y = \left(\frac{m - 2}{2}\right) x^2 + \left(\frac{-m + 4}{2}\right) x,$$

where x is the number of the figurate number (1st, 2d, etc.). Therefore, for the nth figurate number, we get

$$y = \left(\frac{m - 2}{2}\right) n^2 + \left(\frac{-m + 4}{2}\right) n$$
$$= n \left[\left(\frac{m - 2}{2}\right) n + \left(\frac{-m + 4}{2}\right)\right]$$
$$= \frac{n\left[(m - 2)n - (m - 4)\right]}{2}$$

This is the same expression we got from Project 8. We have shown that we get the same thing going both ways (across and down).

Tessellations

E. JUDITH CANTEY

Imagine that you have an infinite supply of jigsaw puzzle pieces, all identical. If it is possible to fit them together without gaps or overlaps to cover the entire plane, the piece is said to tile the plane, and the resulting pattern is called a tessellation. From the most ancient times such tessellations have been used throughout the world for floor and wall coverings and as patterns for furniture, rugs, tapestries, quilts, clothing and other objects.

Martin Gardner

THE purpose of your work in this unit is to acquaint you with the terminology of transformations, to introduce you to the fascinating drawings of tessellations of the Escher type, to offer an explanation of the mathematics underlying the drawings, and to give you the opportunity to create your own imaginative pattern.

Projects

Project 1

Write a short history of the uses of tessellations (250 words).

Guide: Reference 1 includes a brief history. Any large encyclopedia should include information on Sumerian mosaics, Moslem and Islamic tile patterns (the Alhambra and the Taj Mahal), Roman tessellae, and more recently, the artwork of the Dutch artist M. C. Escher. (Other possibilities: Chinese lattice, Hungarian crochet, African design, and American quilt patterns.)

Project 2

Define each of the following terms: symmetric, transformation, translation (slide), rotation (turn), reflection (flip), tessellation, glide-reflection, line symmetry, point symmetry, regular polygon, polygonal tessellation, regular tessellation, semiregular tessellation, nonregular tessellation, demiregular tessellation, full-turn, half-turn.

Guide: Use References 1 and 4–8 for this project. References 5 and 6 will be very helpful. A knowledge of the terminology will be useful in describing symmetries and studying the tessellations encountered.

Polyominoes are shapes formed by joining a certain number of congruent squares so that any two squares in the shape are completely connected on at least one side. It is possible to tile the plane using one or more polyomino shapes. Three types of polyominoes are these:

- **Tetrominoes**— four congruent squares; four possible arrangements, each of which will tile the plane. Figures 1 and 2 are tessellations with tetrominoes.
- **Pentominoes**—five congruent squares; twelve possible arrangements, each of which will tile the plane. Figures 3 and 4 are tessellations with pentominoes.
- **Hexominoes**— six congruent squares; thirty-five possible arrangements, each of which will tile the plane. Figures 5 and 6 are tessellations with hexominoes.

Project 3

Answer each of the following questions for each figure (1–6):

1. Can the figure be translated to produce the same design? (Draw dotted lines to indicate the direction of translation that produces the exact image.)

2. Can the figure be translated to produce a color change symmetry? (Draw dashed lines to indicate a color change direction of translation.)

3. Can the figure be reflected to produce an identical design? (Draw a zigzag line to indicate the axis of reflection.)

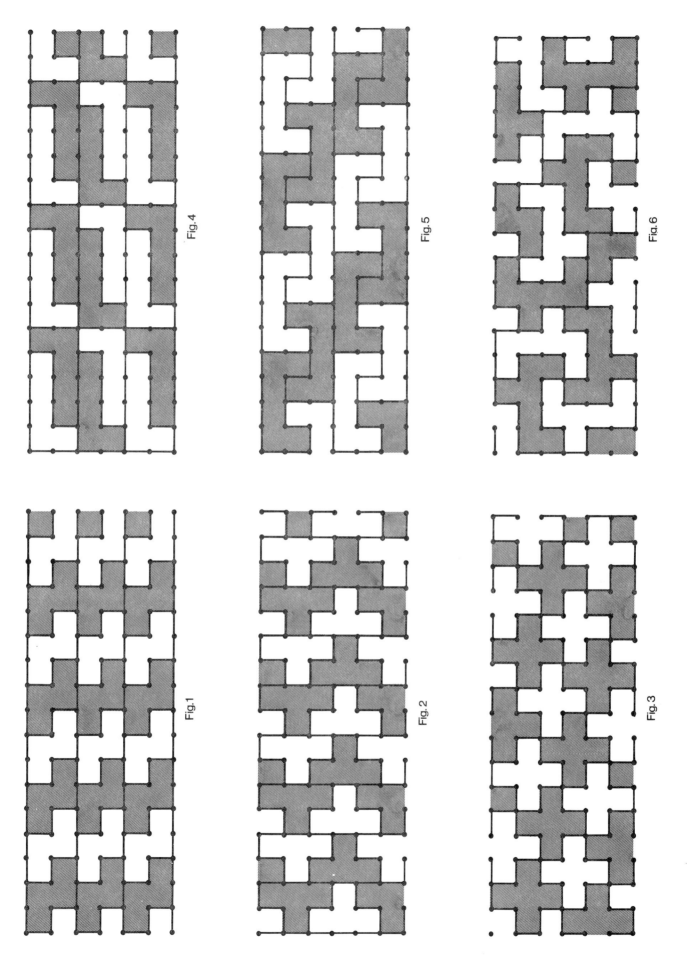

Fig.1

Fig.2

Fig.3

Fig.4

Fig.5

Fig.6

4. Can color change symmetry be obtained by reflection? (Use a heavy, solid line to mark the axis of reflection.)

5. Can the design be rotated about a point to produce an exact image? (Mark the point(s) with a small circle.)

6. Can the design be rotated about a point to produce a color change symmetry? (Mark the point(s) with an asterisk.)

7. Does the figure have glide-reflection symmetry?

Project 4

I often wondered at my own mania for making periodic drawings. . . . What can be the reason of my being alone in this field? Why does none of my fellow-artists seem to be fascinated as I am by these interlocking shapes?

M. C. Escher

Study selected tessellations of the Escher type, select one, and determine if it possesses translation, reflection, rotation, or glide-reflection symmetry. Answer the same questions listed in Project 3.

Guide: References 4, 6, and 7 are excellent. Reference 9 has a limited number of samples.

Project 5

Create an original tessellation of the Escher type.

Guide: References 4, 6, and 8 will guide you through a step-by-step procedure for creating a tessellation. Reference 9 or other geometry texts may offer suggestions on how to proceed.

In order to create recognizable figures, you should first experiment with the alteration of a triangle, quadrilateral, or hexagon. Look at the new figure and try to visualize boundaries of familiar objects. Once you have an idea of what the shape might represent, the next step is to modify the shape to look more like what you imagine it to be.

Another approach is to visualize an object from the shape of the polygon, then modify it to create the desired result.

Creating drawings of the Escher type requires involvement through active participation. Practice, trial and error, and self-discovery will make your creations more rewarding.

Further Investigations

If you are interested in this topic, you may wish to investigate the mathematical proofs for the types of polygons that tile the plane (References 2 and 3). Combinatorics is a branch of mathematics that deals with the study of this type of problem and its solution.

REFERENCES

1. Bezuska, Stanley, Margaret Kenney, and Linda Silvey. *Tessellations: The Geometry of Patterns.* Palo Alto, Calif.: Creative Publications, 1977.

2. Gardner, Martin. "On Tessellating the Plane with Convex Polygon Tiles." *Scientific American,* July 1975, pp. 112–17.

3. Gardner, Martin. "More about Tiling the Plane: The Possibilities of Polyominoes, Polyiamonds and Polyhexes." *Scientific American,* August 1975, pp. 112–15.

4. Haak, Sheila. "Transformation Geometry and the Artwork of M. C. Escher." *Mathematics Teacher* 69 (December 1976):647–52.

5. Maletsky, Evan M. "Designs with Tessellations." *Mathematics Teacher* 67 (April 1974): 335–38.

6. Ranucci, E. R., and J. L. Teeters. *Creating Escher-Type Drawings.* Palo Alto, Calif.: Creative Publications, 1977.

7. Ranucci, Ernest R. "Master of Tessellations: M. C. Escher, 1898-1972." *Mathematics Teacher* 67 (April 1974):299–306.

8. Teeters, Joseph L. "How to Draw Tessellations of the Escher Type." *Mathematics Teacher* 67 (April 1974):307–10.

9. Wells, David W., LeRoy C. Dalton, and Vincent F. Brunner. *Using Geometry.* 2d ed. Minichapter, "Repeating Designs." River Forest, Ill.: Laidlaw Bros., 1981.

Teacher Notes

Project 1

The design of geometric shapes that individually or in combination cover a flat surface without gaps or overlappings has a long history. About 4000 B.C., the Sumerians, in the Mesopotamian Valley, built homes and temples decorated with mosaics in geometric patterns. The materials used in the mosaics were thin slabs of burned clay, called tiles. Colored or glazed tiles served not only as part of the structure of buildings but also as artistic decorations.

Roman buildings, floors, and pavements were decorated with tiles that the Romans called *tessellae*. These designs influenced a modern Dutch artist, M. C. Escher. He saw the possibility of covering a surface with a repeating design of animals or people.

Later, the Persians and the Moors showed that they were masters of tile decoration. About seven hundred years ago, repeating designs were used to decorate the Alhambra, a palace in Spain. The Moors used congruent, multicolored tiles on the walls and floors of their buildings. Moslem and Islamic tile patterns with striking colors still survive.

Project 2 (Definitions)

Symmetric. A figure is symmetric if and only if there exists some transformation (but not the identity transformation) that maps the figure onto itself.

Transformation. A correspondence or matching between points of the plane.

Translation (slide). A linear shift or slide of the figure in the plane.

Rotation (turn). Turning the figure about a given point in the plane.

Reflection (flip). Flipping points or figures about a line in the plane.

Tessellation. A complete covering of a plane by one or more figures in a repeating pattern with no overlapping of figures.

Glide-reflection. A linear shift and a flipping about a line in the plane.

Line symmetry. When each point in the figure can be reflected into the figure through the line.

Point symmetry. A half-turn about the point that makes the figure coincide with itself (also called radial symmetry).

n-fold symmetry. A figure that coincides with itself when rotated through an angle of $360°/n$ about its point of symmetry.

Regular polygon. A polygon with equal sides and equal angles.

Polygonal tessellation. A tessellation with polygons.

Regular tessellation. A tessellation of the plane that covers the plane with repetitions of one particular regular polygon.

Semiregular tessellation. A tessellation of the plane with a combination of two or more kinds of regular polygons arranged so that every vertex is congruent to every other vertex.

Nonregular tessellation. A tessellation with nonregular, simple convex and concave polygons.

Demiregular tessellation. A tessellation that includes a combination of two or three vertex types with regular polygons.

Full-turn. A complete rotation through 360° about a point.

Half-turn. A rotation through 180°.

Project 3 (See the following figures.)

Projects 4 and 5 will have solutions that vary.

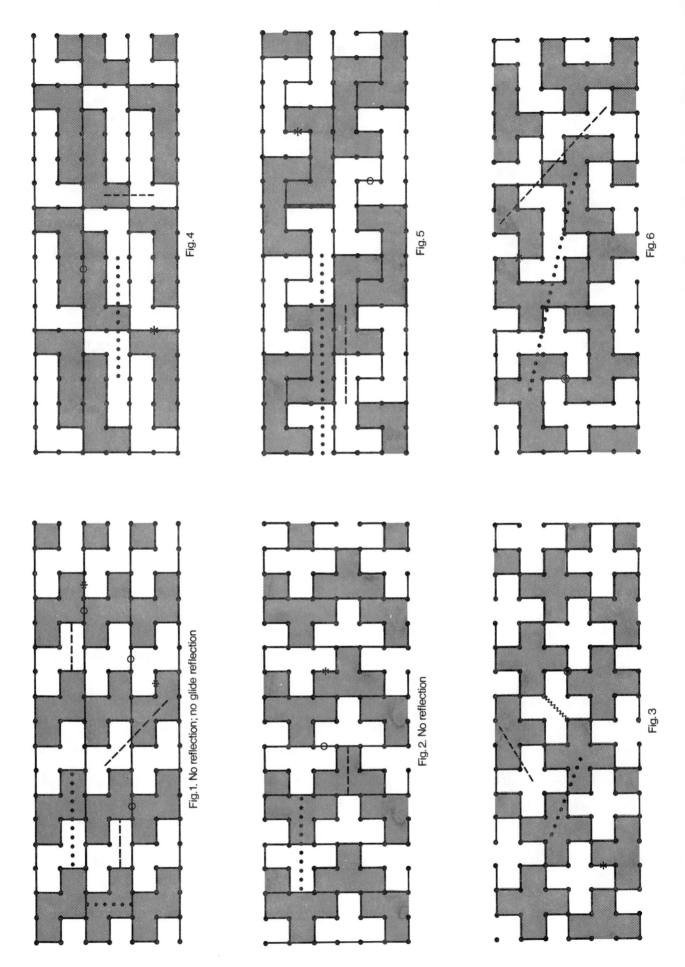

Fig. 4

Fig. 5

Fig. 6

Fig. 1. No reflection; no glide reflection

Fig. 2. No reflection

Fig. 3

Transformations and Matrices with Applications

JOHN HUBER

T RANSFORMATIONS as used in this unit are simply mappings of points in a plane into points in a plane. For example, if every point in a plane is moved three places to the right, the transformation is called a *horizontal translation*. Since there is a one-to-one correspondence between points in the plane and their coordinates, we shall write the effect of a transformation by stating the effect on the coordinates of the point.

A matrix is a convenient mathematical tool for representing transformations of coordinates. In your study of algebra, you probably considered a matrix as a rectangular array of numbers. Initially in this unit, matrices will be used to represent certain types of transformations of the plane called *linear transformations*. Then, applications of matrices to circular functions and complex numbers will be examined. Finally, the determinant of a matrix as it relates to a transformation will be examined.

Projects

Project 1

Identify each of the following transformations: reflection in a line, rotations about the origin that are multiples of 90°, shears parallel to the x- and y-axes, size transformations, stretch transformations, and orthogonal projections onto the x- and y-axes. Complete the following exercises.

1. Find the image of $\triangle ABC$ where $A = (0, 0)$, $B = (2, 0)$, and $C = (2, 1)$ under each of the following transformations, then describe the effect of the transformation in words.

a) $T(x, y) = (-x, y)$	f) $T(x, y) = (x + y, y)$
b) $T(x, y) = (2x, 2y)$	g) $T(x, y) = (x, 3y)$
c) $T(x, y) = (x, -y)$	h) $T(x, y) = (0, y)$
d) $T(x, y) = (-y, x)$	i) $T(x, y) = (x, 2x + y)$
e) $T(x, y) = (x, 0)$	j) $T(x, y) = (y, -x)$

Guide: References 1, 2, 3, and 9 will be helpful.

2. Write an algebraic expression that describes each of the following transformations:

a) A reflection over the x-axis

b) A rotation of 180° centered at the origin

c) A size transformation of magnitude 3 centered at the origin

d) A rotation of 90° counterclockwise about the origin

e) A vertical stretch transformation of magnitude 2

3. Find the composite $T \circ S$ and $S \circ T$ for each of the following:

a) $S(x, y) = (x, -y) \quad T(x, y) = (2x, 2y)$

b) $S(x, y) = (-y, x) \quad T(x, y) = (3x, y)$

c) $S(x, y) = (x, x + y) \quad T(x, y) = (x + 2y, y)$

d) $S(x, y) = (x, 2y) \quad T(x, y) = (2x, y)$

e) Does $T \circ S = S \circ T$ for all transformations S and T?

Guide: Let S and T be transformations. The transformation that maps (x, y) onto $T[S(x, y)]$ is called the *composite* of S and T, and is written $T \circ S$. The operation $\circ$ is called *composition*.

Example: Let $S(x, y) = (-x, y)$ and $T(x, y) = (-y, x)$.

Then $T \circ S(x, y) = T[S(x, y)]$
$$= T(-x, y)$$
$$= (-y, -x)$$

Project 2

Write a 2 × 2 matrix representation for a given transformation. To satisfy this requirement, complete the following exercises.

Guide: References 4, 8, and 10 will be helpful. Note that you need to know only what happens to (1, 0) and (0, 1) under the transformation. If you need to review matrix operations, consult References 5, 8, and 10.

1. Write a 2 × 2 matrix representation for each of the following transformations:

a) $T(x, y) = (2x, \frac{1}{2}y)$ d) $T(x, y) = (2x + y, x - 2y)$
b) $T(x, y) = (x + y, y)$ e) $T(x, y) = (x, y)$
c) $T(x, y) = (-y, x)$

2. Suppose the matrix representations of S, T, and U are

$$\begin{bmatrix} 0 & 1 \\ 1 & 0 \end{bmatrix}, \begin{bmatrix} 2 & 0 \\ 0 & 2 \end{bmatrix}, \text{ and } \begin{bmatrix} 1 & -2 \\ 3 & 4 \end{bmatrix}, \text{ respectively.}$$

Write the matrix associated with each of the following:

a) $S \circ T$ d) $T \circ U$
b) $T \circ S$ e) $S \circ (T \circ U)$
c) $S \circ U$

Guide: If M is the matrix representation for a transformation S, and N is the matrix representation for a transformation T, then the product $N \cdot M$ is the matrix representation for the composition $T \circ S$.

Example: Let $S(x, y) = (-y, x)$ and $T = (2x + y, y - x)$.

$$T \quad \circ \quad S(x, y) = T(S(x, y)) = T(-y, x) = (x - 2y, x + y)$$
$$\updownarrow \qquad \updownarrow$$
$$\begin{bmatrix} 2 & 1 \\ -1 & 1 \end{bmatrix}\begin{bmatrix} 0 & -1 \\ 1 & 0 \end{bmatrix}\begin{bmatrix} x \\ y \end{bmatrix} = \begin{bmatrix} 1 & -2 \\ 1 & 1 \end{bmatrix}\begin{bmatrix} x \\ y \end{bmatrix} = \begin{bmatrix} x - 2y \\ x + y \end{bmatrix}$$

3. Let $M = \begin{bmatrix} a & c \\ b & d \end{bmatrix}$ be the matrix representation of the transformation T.

a) Show that $T(1, 0) = (a, b)$ c) Show that $T(0, 0) = (0, 0)$
b) Show that $T(0, 1) = (c, d)$ d) Show that $T(x, y) = (ax + cy, bx + dy)$

Project 3

Examine the relationship between the matrix representation of a rotation about the origin and circular functions. To satisfy this requirement, complete the following exercises.

Guide: References 8 and 10 will help you. Let θ be the magnitude of a rotation about the origin. Then the cosine and sine of θ can be defined as the first and second coordinates of the image of (1, 0) under this rotation, respectively. Using this as our starting point, all the usual properties of the sine and cosine functions can be developed.

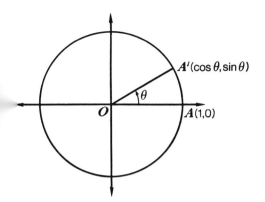

1. Let $O = (0, 0)$, $A = (1, 0)$, and $B = (0, 1)$. If the image of A is $A' = (\cos \theta, \sin \theta)$, then the image of B' must be such that $m \angle A'OB'$ is 90°. Using the matrix representation for a 90° counterclockwise rotation, show that $B' = (-\sin \theta, \cos \theta)$. Then conclude that the matrix representation of a rotation of magnitude θ about the origin is

$$\begin{bmatrix} \cos \theta & -\sin \theta \\ \sin \theta & \cos \theta \end{bmatrix}$$

2. Let r_x, r_y, and $r_{x=y}$ denote reflections over the x-axis, y-axis, and the line $y = x$, respectively. Let R_θ and $R_{-\theta}$ denote rotations about the origin with magnitude θ and $-\theta$, respectively. Using the figure below, show each of the following:

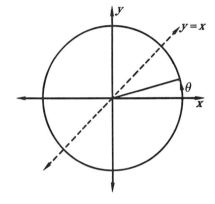

a) Using $R_{-\theta}(1, 0) = r_x \circ R_\theta(1, 0)$, show that $(\cos(-\theta), \sin(-\theta)) = (\cos \theta, -\sin \theta)$. That is,

$$\cos(-\theta) = \cos \theta$$
$$\sin(-\theta) = -\sin \theta.$$

b) Using $R_{90°-\theta}(1, 0) = r_{y=x} \circ R_\theta(1, 0)$, show that $(\cos(90° - \theta), \sin(90° - \theta)) = (\sin \theta, \cos \theta)$. That is,

$$\cos(90° - \theta) = \sin \theta$$
$$\sin(90° - \theta) = \cos \theta.$$

c) Using $R_{180°-\theta}(1, 0) = r_{y\text{-axis}} \circ R_\theta(1, 0)$, show that $(\cos(180° - \theta), \sin(180° - \theta)) = (-\cos \theta, \sin \theta)$. That is,

$$\cos(180° - \theta) = -\cos \theta$$
$$\sin(180° - \theta) = \sin \theta.$$

d) Using the same reasoning as in problems 1–3, find expressions for each of the following in terms of $\cos \theta$ and $\sin \theta$:

- $\cos(90° + \theta)$
- $\sin(90° + \theta)$

- $\cos(180° + \theta)$
- $\sin(180° + \theta)$

3. Let $R_\theta = \begin{bmatrix} \cos \theta & -\sin \theta \\ \sin \theta & \cos \theta \end{bmatrix}$ and $R_\phi = \begin{bmatrix} \cos \phi & -\sin \phi \\ \sin \phi & \cos \phi \end{bmatrix}$.

Using the fact that a rotation of magnitude θ followed by a rotation of magnitude ϕ about the origin is the same as a rotation of magnitude $\theta + \phi$ about the origin, show that

$$\cos(\theta + \phi) = \cos \theta \cos \phi - \sin \theta \sin \phi$$
$$\sin(\theta + \phi) = \sin \theta \cos \phi + \cos \theta \sin \phi.$$

Hint: Let $R_{\theta+\phi} = \begin{bmatrix} \cos(\theta+\phi) & -\sin(\theta+\phi) \\ \sin(\theta+\phi) & \cos(\theta+\phi) \end{bmatrix}$.

Using the fact that $R_\phi \cdot R_\theta = R_{\theta+\phi}$, multiply the matrices together and set corresponding entries equal to each other.

Project 4

Describe the relationship between the determinant of a 2 × 2 matrix and the change in area of a figure under a transformation represented by a 2 × 2 matrix. To satisfy this requirement complete the following exercises.

Guide: References 1 and 8 will be helpful. The determinant of a 2 × 2 matrix represents the signed area of the image of the unit square $ABCD$, where $A = (0, 0)$, $B = (1, 0)$, $C = (1, 1)$, and $D = (0, 1)$ under the transformation represented by the 2 × 2 matrix. By signed area we mean—

- the area of the unit square $ABCD$ is one;
- the signed area is reversed if the orientation is reversed; and
- the signed area of two nonoverlapping figures is the sum of the separate signed areas.

In this section, we will examine the relationship between determinants of matrices and the signed area that is represented.

1. Define the determinant of the matrix $\begin{bmatrix} a & c \\ b & d \end{bmatrix}$ to be $ad - bc$. We will denote the determinant

of $\begin{bmatrix} a & c \\ b & d \end{bmatrix}$ by $\det \begin{bmatrix} a & c \\ b & d \end{bmatrix}$.

a) Show $\det \begin{bmatrix} 1 & 0 \\ 0 & 1 \end{bmatrix} = 1$.

c) Show $\det \begin{bmatrix} a & kc \\ b & kd \end{bmatrix} = k \det \begin{bmatrix} a & c \\ b & d \end{bmatrix}$.

b) Show $\det \begin{bmatrix} ka & c \\ kb & d \end{bmatrix} = k \det \begin{bmatrix} a & c \\ b & d \end{bmatrix}$.

d) Show $\det \begin{bmatrix} a & c \\ b & d \end{bmatrix} = -\det \begin{bmatrix} c & a \\ d & b \end{bmatrix}$.

e) Show $\det \begin{bmatrix} a_1 + a_2 & c \\ b_1 + b_2 & d \end{bmatrix} = \det \begin{bmatrix} a_1 & c \\ b_1 & d \end{bmatrix} + \det \begin{bmatrix} a_2 & c \\ b_2 & d \end{bmatrix}$.

2. Let $ABCD$ be the unit square with vertices $A = (0, 0)$, $B = (1, 0)$, $C = (1, 1)$, and $D = (0, 1)$. Let $M = \begin{bmatrix} a & c \\ b & d \end{bmatrix}$ be the matrix representation of the transformation T, where $T(x, y) = (ax + cy, bx + dy)$. Show $T(A) = A'$, $T(B) = B'$, $T(C) = C'$, and $T(D) = D'$, where $A' = (0, 0)$, $B' = (a, b)$, $C' = (a + c, b + d)$, and $D' = (c, d)$.

3. Let $M = \begin{bmatrix} 1 & 0 \\ k & 1 \end{bmatrix}$, where $k > 0$, be the matrix representation of the transformation T, where $T(x, y) = (x, kx + y)$.

a) Show that $T(A) = A'$, $T(B) = B'$, $T(C) = C'$, and $T(D) = D'$, where $A' = (0, 0)$, $B' = (1, k)$, $C' = (1, k + 1)$, and $D' = (0, 1)$.

b) Show that the area of $A'B'C'D'$ is one square unit. [*Hint:* Using $A'D'$ as the base of the parallelogram, what is the height of $A'B'C'D'$?]

4. Let $A = (0, 0)$, $B = (a, b)$, $C = (c, d)$, and $D = (a + c, b + d)$. Let $M = \begin{bmatrix} 1 & 0 \\ k & 1 \end{bmatrix}$, where $k = -\dfrac{c}{a}$ and $a \neq 0$ be the matrix representation of the transformation T.

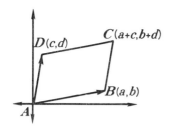 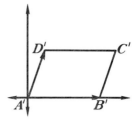

a) Show that $T(A) = A'$, $T(B) = B'$, $T(C) = C'$, and $T(D) = D'$, where $A' = (0, 0)$, $B' = (a, 0)$,
$C' = \left(a + b, \ -\left(\dfrac{c}{a}\right)b + d\right)$, and $D' = \left(b, -\left(\dfrac{c}{a}\right)b + d\right)$

b) Show that the area of $A'B'C'D'$ is $ad - bc$, and as a result the area of $ABCD$ is $ad - bc$.

5. Using the results of the preceding problem, we can conclude that the area of a figure under a transformation with a matrix representation M changes by a scale factor $|\det(M)|$. If $\det(M) > 0$ the orientation remains unchanged, and if $\det(M) < 0$ the orientation is reversed.

Let $A = (x_1, y_1)$, $B = (x_2, y_2)$, $C = (x_3, y_3)$, and $O = (0, 0)$. Show that

$$\text{Area}(\triangle ABC) = \frac{1}{2}\left| \det\begin{bmatrix} x_1 & x_2 \\ y_1 & y_2 \end{bmatrix} + \det\begin{bmatrix} x_2 & x_3 \\ y_2 & y_3 \end{bmatrix} + \det\begin{bmatrix} x_3 & x_1 \\ y_3 & y_1 \end{bmatrix} \right|.$$

[*Hint*: Area $(\triangle ABC)$ = Area $(\triangle OBC)$ − Area $(\triangle OBA)$ − Area $(\triangle OAC)$.]

6. Use the result of the previous problem to show that the area of the convex polygon $A_1 A_2 \ldots A_n$, where $A_k = (x_k, y_k)$, is given by

$$\frac{1}{2}\left| \det\begin{bmatrix} x_1 & x_2 \\ y_1 & y_2 \end{bmatrix} + \det\begin{bmatrix} x_2 & x_3 \\ y_2 & y_3 \end{bmatrix} + \cdots + \det\begin{bmatrix} x_{n-1} & x_n \\ y_{n-1} & y_n \end{bmatrix} + \det\begin{bmatrix} x_n & x_1 \\ y_n & y_2 \end{bmatrix} \right|.$$

Further Investigations

Examine the relationship between the geometry of complex number multiplication and the matrix operations for size transformations and rotations about the origin. To complete this project, complete the following exercises.

Guide: References 8 and 10 will be helpful. Instead of representing complex numbers as the ordered pair (a, b) or in the form $a + bi$, in this unit we will examine complex numbers represented by a matrix $\begin{bmatrix} a & -b \\ b & a \end{bmatrix}$, which is the composition of a size transformation and a rotation.

$$\text{Let } R = \begin{bmatrix} \cos\theta & -\sin\theta \\ \sin\theta & \cos\theta \end{bmatrix} \text{ and } S = \begin{bmatrix} k & 0 \\ 0 & k \end{bmatrix}.$$

1. Show that $R \cdot S = S \cdot R$.

2. Show that if $S \circ R = Z$, where $Z = \begin{bmatrix} a & b \\ b & a \end{bmatrix}$, then $k = \sqrt{a^2 + b^2}$,

$\cos\theta = \dfrac{a}{\sqrt{a^2 + b^2}}$, and $\sin\theta = \dfrac{b}{\sqrt{a^2 + b^2}}$.

3. Let $M = \left\{ \begin{bmatrix} a & -b \\ b & a \end{bmatrix} \middle| a, b \in R \right\}$.

Show that $(M, +, \cdot)$ is a field where addition and multiplication are matrix addition and matrix multiplication.

4. Let $\begin{bmatrix} a & -b \\ b & a \end{bmatrix}$ be the matrix associated with the complex number $a + bi$ where $i^2 = -1$.

a) Show that the matrix associated with the complex number $(a + bi) + (c + di)$

is the matrix $\begin{bmatrix} a & -b \\ b & a \end{bmatrix} + \begin{bmatrix} c & -d \\ d & c \end{bmatrix}$.

b) Show that the matrix associated with the complex number $(a + bi)(c + di)$ is the matrix.

$$\begin{bmatrix} a & -b \\ b & a \end{bmatrix} \begin{bmatrix} c & -d \\ d & c \end{bmatrix}$$

5. Let $R = \begin{bmatrix} \cos \theta & -\sin \theta \\ \sin \theta & \cos \theta \end{bmatrix}$.

   a) Show: $R^2 = \begin{bmatrix} \cos 2\theta & -\sin 2\theta \\ \sin 2\theta & \cos 2\theta \end{bmatrix}$

   b) Show: $R^n = \begin{bmatrix} \cos n\theta & -\sin n\theta \\ \sin n\theta & \cos n\theta \end{bmatrix}$

6. Let $S = \begin{bmatrix} k & 0 \\ 0 & k \end{bmatrix}$.

   a) Show: $S^2 = \begin{bmatrix} k^2 & 0 \\ 0 & k^2 \end{bmatrix}$

   b) Show: $S^n = \begin{bmatrix} k^n & 0 \\ 0 & k^n \end{bmatrix}$

7. Let $R = \begin{bmatrix} \cos \theta & -\sin \theta \\ \sin \theta & \cos \theta \end{bmatrix}$ and $S = \begin{bmatrix} k & 0 \\ 0 & k \end{bmatrix}$.

   a) Show: $(SR)^2 = \begin{bmatrix} k^2 \cos 2\theta & -k^2 \sin 2\theta \\ k^2 \sin 2\theta & k^2 \cos 2\theta \end{bmatrix}$

   b) Show: $(SR)^n = \begin{bmatrix} k^n \cos n\theta & -k^n \sin n\theta \\ k^n \sin n\theta & k^n \cos n\theta \end{bmatrix}$

8. Using the results of the previous problems, show that if $z = k(\cos \theta + i \sin \theta)$, then $z^n = k^n(\cos n\theta + i \sin n\theta)$.

9. Let $R = \begin{bmatrix} \cos \theta & -\sin \theta \\ \sin \theta & \cos \theta \end{bmatrix}$.

   a) Show that $R_0 = \begin{bmatrix} \cos\left(\dfrac{\theta}{2}\right) & -\sin\left(\dfrac{\theta}{2}\right) \\ \sin\left(\dfrac{\theta}{2}\right) & \cos\left(\dfrac{\theta}{2}\right) \end{bmatrix}$

   and $R_1 = \begin{bmatrix} \cos\left(\dfrac{\theta + 2\pi}{2}\right) & -\sin\left(\dfrac{\theta + 2\pi}{2}\right) \\ \sin\left(\dfrac{\theta + 2\pi}{2}\right) & \cos\left(\dfrac{\theta + 2\pi}{2}\right) \end{bmatrix}$

   are solutions to the matrix equation $R^2 = I$, where

   $$I = \begin{bmatrix} 1 & 0 \\ 0 & 1 \end{bmatrix}.$$

   b) Show that each of $R_m = \begin{bmatrix} \cos\left(\dfrac{\theta + 2\pi m}{n}\right) & -\sin\left(\dfrac{\theta + 2\pi m}{n}\right) \\ \sin\left(\dfrac{\theta + 2\pi m}{n}\right) & \cos\left(\dfrac{\theta + 2\pi m}{n}\right) \end{bmatrix}$

   for $m = 0, 1, 2, \ldots, n - 1$ are solutions to the matrix equation $R^n = I$.

10. Let $S = \begin{bmatrix} k & 0 \\ 0 & k \end{bmatrix}$ and $R = \begin{bmatrix} \cos\theta & -\sin \\ \sin\theta & \cos \end{bmatrix}$ and $M = SR$.

a) Show that $M_0 = \begin{bmatrix} \sqrt{k}\cos\left(\dfrac{\theta}{2}\right) & -\sqrt{k}\sin\left(\dfrac{\theta}{2}\right) \\ \sqrt{k}\sin\left(\dfrac{\theta}{2}\right) & \sqrt{k}\cos\left(\dfrac{\theta}{2}\right) \end{bmatrix}$

and $M_1 = \begin{bmatrix} \sqrt{k}\cos\left(\dfrac{\theta+2\pi}{2}\right) & -\sqrt{k}\sin\left(\dfrac{\theta+2\pi}{2}\right) \\ \sqrt{k}\sin\left(\dfrac{\theta+2\pi}{2}\right) & \sqrt{k}\cos\left(\dfrac{\theta+2\pi}{2}\right) \end{bmatrix}$

are solutions to the matrix equation $M^2 = I$.

b) Show that each of

$$M_m = \begin{bmatrix} \sqrt[m]{k}\cos\left(\dfrac{\theta+2\pi m}{n}\right) & -\sqrt[m]{k}\sin\left(\dfrac{\theta+2\pi m}{n}\right) \\ \sqrt[m]{k}\sin\left(\dfrac{\theta+2\pi m}{n}\right) & \sqrt[m]{k}\cos\left(\dfrac{\theta+2\pi m}{n}\right) \end{bmatrix}$$

for $m = 0, 1, 2, \ldots, n-1$ is a solution to the matrix equation $M^n = I$.

11. Using the results of the previous problems show that if $z = k(\cos\theta + i\sin\theta)$, then each of

$$z_0 = \sqrt[n]{k}\left[\cos\left(\frac{\theta}{n}\right) + i\sin\left(\frac{\theta}{n}\right)\right]$$

$$z_1 = \sqrt[n]{k}\left[\cos\left(\frac{\theta+2\pi}{n}\right) + i\sin\left(\frac{\theta+2\pi}{n}\right)\right]$$

$$\vdots$$

$$z_m = \sqrt[n]{k}\left[\cos\left(\frac{\theta+2\pi m}{n}\right) + i\sin\left(\frac{\theta+2\pi m}{n}\right)\right]$$

for $m = 0, 1, \ldots, n-1$ is a solution to the complex number equation $z^n = 1$.

REFERENCES

1. Coxford, Arthur, and Zalman P. Usiskin. *Geometry: A Transformation Approach*. River Forest, Ill.: Laidlaw Brothers, 1975.
2. Jackson, Stanley B. "Applications of Transformations to Topics in Elementary Geometry: Part I." *Mathematics Teacher* 68 (1975):554–62.
3. Jackson, Stanley B. "Applications of Transformations to Topics in Elementary Geometry: Part II." *Mathematics Teacher* 68 (1975):630–35.
4. Swadener, Marc. "On Transformations and Matrices." *Two-Year College Mathematics Journal* 4 (1973):44–51.
5. Travers, Kenneth J., LeRoy C. Dalton, and Vincent F. Brunner. *Using Advanced Algebra*. 3d ed. River Forest, Ill.: Laidlaw Brothers, 1981.
6. Usiskin, Zalman. "Applications of Group and Isomorphic Groups to Topics in the Standard Curriculum, Grades 9–11: Part I." *Mathematics Teacher* 68 (1975):99–106.
7. Usiskin, Zalman. "Applications of Groups and Isomorphic Groups to Topics in the Standard Curriculum, Grades 9–11: Part II." *Mathematics Teacher* 68 (1975):234–46.
8. Usiskin, Zalman. *Advanced Algebra with Transformations and Applications*. River Forest, Ill.: Laidlaw Brothers, 1976.
9. Wells, David W., LeRoy C. Dalton, and Vincent F. Brunner. *Using Geometry*. River Forest, Ill.: Laidlaw Brothers, 1981.
10. Wooten, William, Edwin F. Beckenbach, O. Lexton Buchanan, Jr., and Mary P. Dolciani. *Modern Trigonometry*. Rev. ed. Boston: Houghton Mifflin Co., 1976.

Teacher Notes

Transformations as used in this unit are simply mappings of points in a plane into points in a plane. These transformations will be represented using the function notation $T(x, y) = (x', y')$, where the point whose coordinate is (x, y) maps onto the point whose coordinate is (x', y') under the transformation T.

After working with the function notation, the transition to representing transformations of the form $T(x, y) = (ax + cy, bx + dy)$ to

$$\begin{bmatrix} a & c \\ b & d \end{bmatrix} \begin{bmatrix} x \\ y \end{bmatrix} = \begin{bmatrix} x' \\ y' \end{bmatrix}$$

is made. Then, these linear transformations are applied to circular functions and complex numbers. Finally, the geometry of the determinant of a matrix representing a linear transformation is examined.

Project 1

Given an algebraic expression for the following transformations, identify the transformation and the converse: reflection in a line, rotations about the origin that are multiples of 90°, shears parallel to x- and y-axes, size transformations, stretch transformations, and orthogonal projections onto x- and y-axes.

This project is intended to have the student translate from an algebraic description to a geometrical description and the converse. It is important that a student interpret expressions like $T(x, y) = (y, x)$ as interchanging the first and second coordinates. Similarly, $T(x, y) = (2x + y, x - 2y)$ should be read as the first coordinate of the image is given by twice the first coordinate of the preimage plus the second coordinate of the preimage, and the second coordinate of the image is the first coordinate of the preimage minus twice the coordinate of the preimage.

The composition of transformations is the same as composition of functions. Thus, $S \circ T(x, y) = (x', y')$ should be read as "T followed by S."

1.

a)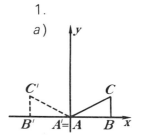

Reflection over y-axis

b)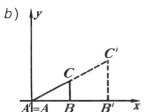

Size transformation centered at origin with magnitude 2

c)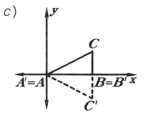

Reflection over x-axis

d)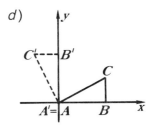

Rotation 90° counterclockwise or 270° clockwise

e)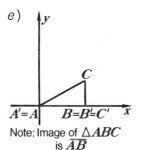

Note: Image of $\triangle ABC$ is $\overline{AB}$

Orthogonal (perpendicular) projection onto x-axis

f)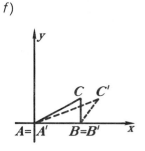

Shear parallel to x-axis

g)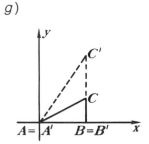

Vertical stretch of magnitude 3

h)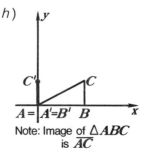

Note: Image of $\triangle ABC$ is $\overline{AC}$

Orthogonal (perpendicular) projection onto y-axis

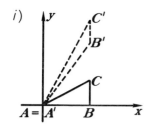

i)

Shear parallel to *y*-axis

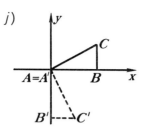

j)

Rotation 270° counterclockwise
or 90° clockwise

2. Write an algebraic expression that describes each of the following transformations:

a) $T(x, y) = (x, -y)$

b) $T(x, y) = (-x, -y)$

c) $T(x, y) = (3x, 3y)$

d) $T(x, y) = (-y, x)$

e) $T(x, y) = (x, 2y)$

3. Find the composite $T \circ S$ and $S \circ T$ for each of the following:

a) $T \circ S(x, y) = T[S(x, y)] = T(x, -y) \quad = (2x, -2y)$
   $S \circ T(x, y) = S[T(x, y)] = S(2x, 2y) \quad = (2x, -2y)$

b) $T \circ S(x, y) = T[S(x, y)] = T(-y, x) \quad = (-3y, x)$
   $S \circ T(x, y) = S[T(x, y)] = S(3x, y) \quad = (-y, 3x)$

c) $T \circ S(x, y) = T[S(x, y)] = T(x, x + y) \quad = (3x + 2y, x + y)$
   $S \circ T(x, y) = S[T(x, y)] = S(x + 2y, y) = (x + 2y, x + 3y)$

d) $T \circ S(x, y) = T[S(x, y)] = T(x, 2y) \quad = (2x, 2y)$
   $S \circ T(x, y) = S[T(x, y)] = S(2x, y) \quad = (2x, 2y)$

e) $T \circ S \neq S \circ T$ for all S and T; see (*b*) and (*c*) above.

Project 2

Write a 2 × 2 matrix representation for a given transformation.

The important idea here is that the matrix representation for a linear transformation is completely determined by the image of (1, 0) and (0, 1). For example, a rotation of 90° counterclockwise about the origin maps (1, 0) onto (0, 1) and (0, 1) onto (−1, 0). Thus, the matrix representation of $R_{90°}$ is given by

$$R_{90°} = \begin{bmatrix} 0 & -1 \\ 1 & 0 \end{bmatrix}$$

$$\uparrow \qquad \uparrow$$
image   image
of   of
(1, 0)   (0, 1).

In addition, we need to observe that the matrix representation for the composition of transformations is the product of the matrices in the same order. For example,

$$T \quad \circ \quad S \quad (x, y) = (x - 2y, s + y)$$
$$\updownarrow \qquad \updownarrow \qquad \updownarrow \qquad \qquad \updownarrow$$
$$\begin{bmatrix} 2 & 1 \\ -1 & 1 \end{bmatrix} \begin{bmatrix} 0 & -1 \\ 1 & 0 \end{bmatrix} \begin{bmatrix} x \\ y \end{bmatrix} = \begin{bmatrix} x - 2y \\ x + y \end{bmatrix}$$

1. Write a 2 × 2 matrix representation for each of the following transformations:

a) $\begin{bmatrix} 2 & 0 \\ 0 & \frac{1}{2} \end{bmatrix}$
b) $\begin{bmatrix} 1 & 1 \\ 0 & 1 \end{bmatrix}$
c) $\begin{bmatrix} 0 & -1 \\ 1 & 0 \end{bmatrix}$
d) $\begin{bmatrix} 2 & 1 \\ 1 & -2 \end{bmatrix}$
e) $\begin{bmatrix} 1 & 0 \\ 0 & 1 \end{bmatrix}$

2. Write the matrix associated with each of the following:

a) $S \circ T$
$$\begin{bmatrix} 0 & 1 \\ 1 & 0 \end{bmatrix}\begin{bmatrix} 2 & 0 \\ 0 & 2 \end{bmatrix} = \begin{bmatrix} 0 & 2 \\ 2 & 0 \end{bmatrix}$$

c) $S \circ U$
$$\begin{bmatrix} 0 & 1 \\ 1 & 0 \end{bmatrix}\begin{bmatrix} 1 & -2 \\ 3 & 4 \end{bmatrix} = \begin{bmatrix} 3 & 4 \\ 1 & -2 \end{bmatrix}$$

b) $T \circ S$
$$\begin{bmatrix} 2 & 0 \\ 0 & 2 \end{bmatrix}\begin{bmatrix} 1 & 0 \\ 0 & 1 \end{bmatrix} = \begin{bmatrix} 2 & 0 \\ 0 & 2 \end{bmatrix}$$

d) $T \circ U$
$$\begin{bmatrix} 2 & 0 \\ 0 & 2 \end{bmatrix}\begin{bmatrix} 1 & -2 \\ 3 & 4 \end{bmatrix} = \begin{bmatrix} 2 & -4 \\ 6 & 8 \end{bmatrix}$$

e) $S \circ (T \circ U)$
$$\begin{bmatrix} 0 & 1 \\ 1 & 0 \end{bmatrix}\left(\begin{bmatrix} 2 & 0 \\ 0 & 2 \end{bmatrix}\begin{bmatrix} 1 & -2 \\ 3 & 4 \end{bmatrix}\right) = \begin{bmatrix} 0 & 1 \\ 1 & 0 \end{bmatrix}\begin{bmatrix} 2 & -4 \\ 6 & 8 \end{bmatrix} = \begin{bmatrix} 6 & 8 \\ 2 & -4 \end{bmatrix}$$

3. Let $M = \begin{bmatrix} a & c \\ b & d \end{bmatrix}$ be the matrix representation of the transformation T.

a) $\begin{bmatrix} a & c \\ b & d \end{bmatrix}\begin{bmatrix} 1 \\ 0 \end{bmatrix} = \begin{bmatrix} a \\ b \end{bmatrix}$

c) $\begin{bmatrix} a & c \\ b & d \end{bmatrix}\begin{bmatrix} 0 \\ 0 \end{bmatrix} = \begin{bmatrix} 0 \\ 0 \end{bmatrix}$

b) $\begin{bmatrix} a & c \\ b & d \end{bmatrix}\begin{bmatrix} 0 \\ 1 \end{bmatrix} = \begin{bmatrix} c \\ d \end{bmatrix}$

d) $\begin{bmatrix} a & c \\ b & d \end{bmatrix}\begin{bmatrix} x \\ y \end{bmatrix} = \begin{bmatrix} ax + cy \\ bx + dy \end{bmatrix}$

so $T(x, y) = (ax + cy, bx + dy)$.

Project 3

Examine the relationship between the matrix representation of a rotation about the origin and circular functions.

If we let θ denote the magnitude of a rotation about the origin and define the cosine and sine of θ to be the first and second coordinates of the image of (1, 0) under this rotation, all the usual properties of the circular function can be developed. The essential tools are reflections in the x-axis, y-axis, and the line $y = x$; and the matrix for a rotation about the origin. In particular, note how easy the formulas for cos $(\theta + \phi)$ and sin $(\theta + \phi)$ are derived using $R_{\theta+\phi} = R_\theta \circ R_\phi$.

1. Since $m\angle A'OB' = 90°$, then $B' = R_{90°}(A')$. Thus,

$$B' = R_{90°}(A') = \begin{bmatrix} 0 & -1 \\ 1 & 0 \end{bmatrix}\begin{bmatrix} \cos \theta \\ \sin \theta \end{bmatrix} = \begin{bmatrix} -\sin \theta \\ \cos \theta \end{bmatrix}.$$

Then, since $R_\theta(A) = (\cos \theta, \sin \theta)$ and $R_\theta(B) = (-\sin \theta, \cos \theta)$,

$$R_\theta = \begin{bmatrix} \cos \theta & -\sin \theta \\ \sin \theta & \cos \theta \end{bmatrix}.$$

2.

a)

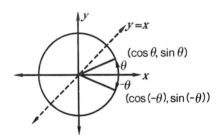

$$R_{-\theta}(1, 0) = \begin{bmatrix} \cos (-\theta) & -\sin (-\theta) \\ \sin (-\theta) & \cos (-\theta) \end{bmatrix}\begin{bmatrix} 1 \\ 0 \end{bmatrix} = \begin{bmatrix} \cos (-\theta) \\ \sin (-\theta) \end{bmatrix}$$

$$r_x \circ R_\theta(1, 0) = \begin{bmatrix} 1 & 0 \\ 0 & -1 \end{bmatrix} \begin{bmatrix} \cos \theta & -\sin \theta \\ \sin \theta & \cos \theta \end{bmatrix} \begin{bmatrix} 1 \\ 0 \end{bmatrix} = \begin{bmatrix} \cos \theta \\ -\sin \theta \end{bmatrix}$$

$$\text{so} \quad \begin{bmatrix} \cos (-\theta) \\ \sin (-\theta) \end{bmatrix} = \begin{bmatrix} \cos \theta \\ -\sin \theta \end{bmatrix}.$$

Therefore,

$$\cos (-\theta) = \cos \theta$$
$$\text{and} \quad \sin (-\theta) = -\sin \theta.$$

b)

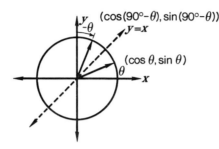

$$R_{90°-\theta}(1, 0) = \begin{bmatrix} \cos (90° - \theta) & -\sin (90° - \theta) \\ \sin (90° - \theta) & \cos (90° - \theta) \end{bmatrix} \begin{bmatrix} 1 \\ 0 \end{bmatrix} = \begin{bmatrix} \cos (90° - \theta) \\ \sin (90° - \theta) \end{bmatrix}$$

$$r_{y=x} \circ R_\theta(1, 0) = \begin{bmatrix} 0 & 1 \\ 1 & 0 \end{bmatrix} \begin{bmatrix} \cos \theta & -\sin \theta \\ \sin \theta & \cos \theta \end{bmatrix} \begin{bmatrix} 1 \\ 0 \end{bmatrix} = \begin{bmatrix} \sin \theta \\ \cos \theta \end{bmatrix}$$

$$\text{so} \quad \begin{bmatrix} \cos (90° - \theta) \\ \sin (90° - \theta) \end{bmatrix} = \begin{bmatrix} \sin \theta \\ \cos \theta \end{bmatrix}.$$

Therefore,

$$\cos (90° - \theta) = \sin \theta$$
$$\text{and} \quad \sin (90° - \theta) = \cos \theta.$$

c)

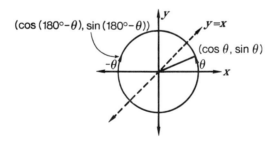

$$R_{180°-\theta}(1, 0) = \begin{bmatrix} \cos (180° - \theta) & -\sin (180° - \theta) \\ \sin (180° - \theta) & \cos (180° - \theta) \end{bmatrix} \begin{bmatrix} 1 \\ 0 \end{bmatrix} = \begin{bmatrix} \cos (180° - \theta) \\ \sin (180° - \theta) \end{bmatrix}$$

$$r_y \circ R_\theta(1, 0) = \begin{bmatrix} -1 & 0 \\ 0 & 1 \end{bmatrix} \begin{bmatrix} \cos \theta & -\sin \theta \\ \sin \theta & \cos \theta \end{bmatrix} \begin{bmatrix} 1 \\ 0 \end{bmatrix} = \begin{bmatrix} -\cos \theta \\ \sin \theta \end{bmatrix}$$

$$\text{so} \quad \begin{bmatrix} \cos (180° - \theta) \\ \sin (180° - \theta) \end{bmatrix} = \begin{bmatrix} -\cos \theta \\ \sin \theta \end{bmatrix}.$$

Therefore,

$$\cos (180° - \theta) = -\cos \theta$$
$$\text{and} \quad \sin (180° - \theta) = \sin \theta.$$

d)

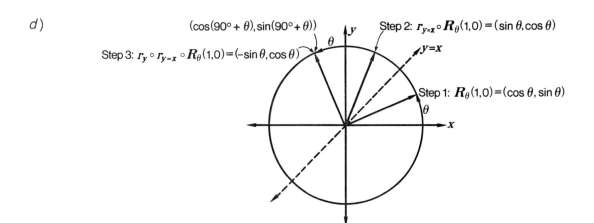

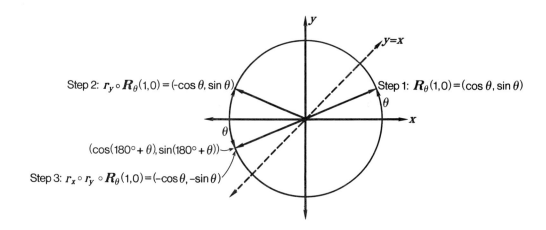

3.

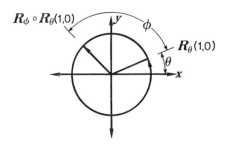

$$R_{\theta+\phi} = R_\theta \circ R_\phi$$

$$\begin{bmatrix} \cos(\theta+\phi) & -\sin(\theta+\phi) \\ \sin(\theta+\phi) & \cos(\theta+\phi) \end{bmatrix} \begin{bmatrix} 1 \\ 0 \end{bmatrix} = \begin{bmatrix} \cos(\theta+\phi) \\ \sin(\theta+\phi) \end{bmatrix}$$

$$\begin{bmatrix} \cos\theta & -\sin\theta \\ \sin\theta & \cos\theta \end{bmatrix} \begin{bmatrix} \cos\phi & -\sin\phi \\ \sin\phi & \cos\phi \end{bmatrix} \begin{bmatrix} 1 \\ 0 \end{bmatrix} = \begin{bmatrix} \cos\theta\cos\phi - \sin\theta\sin\phi \\ \sin\theta\cos\phi + \cos\theta\sin\phi \end{bmatrix}$$

$$\text{so} \quad \begin{bmatrix} \cos(\theta+\phi) \\ \sin(\theta+\phi) \end{bmatrix} = \begin{bmatrix} \cos\theta\cos\phi - \sin\theta\sin\phi \\ \sin\theta\cos\phi + \cos\theta\sin\phi \end{bmatrix}.$$

Therefore,

$$\cos(\theta+\phi) = \cos\theta\cos\phi - \sin\theta\sin\phi$$
$$\text{and} \quad \sin(\theta+\phi) = \sin\theta\cos\phi + \cos\theta\sin\phi.$$

Project 4

Describe the relationship between the determinant of a 2 × 2 matrix and the change in area of a figure under a transformation represented by a 2 × 2 matrix.

The purpose of this project is to have the student see the relationship between a matrix for a transformation and the determinant of the matrix. In particular, the determinant represents the change in signed area under a transformation. Thus,

$$\text{area } (T(\mathscr{R})) = |\det(T)|\,\text{area } (\mathscr{R}),$$

where $\mathscr{R}$ is a plane region. If the determinant is negative, the orientation of the image and preimage are reversed; otherwise the orientation of the image and preimage are the same. The last problem is designed to develop the formula for finding the area of a convex polygon given the coordinates of the vertices.

1.

a) $\det \begin{bmatrix} 1 & 0 \\ 0 & 1 \end{bmatrix} = 1 \cdot 1 - 0 \cdot 0$

b) $\det \begin{bmatrix} ka & c \\ kb & d \end{bmatrix} = ka \cdot d - kb \cdot c$

$= k(ad - bc)$

$= k \det \begin{bmatrix} a & c \\ b & d \end{bmatrix}$

c) $\det \begin{bmatrix} a & kc \\ b & kd \end{bmatrix} = a(kd) - b(kc)$

$= k(ad - bc)$

$= k \det \begin{bmatrix} a & c \\ b & d \end{bmatrix}$

d) $\det \begin{bmatrix} a & c \\ b & d \end{bmatrix} = ad - bc = -(bc - ad) = -\det \begin{bmatrix} a & c \\ b & d \end{bmatrix}$

e) $\det \begin{bmatrix} a_1 + a_2 & c \\ b_1 + b_2 & d \end{bmatrix} = (a_1 + a_2)d - (b_1 + b_2)c$

$= a_1 d + a_2 d - b_1 c - b_2 c$

$= (a_1 d - b_1 c) + (a_2 d - b_2 c)$

$= \det \begin{bmatrix} a_1 & c \\ b_1 & d \end{bmatrix} + \det \begin{bmatrix} a_2 & c \\ b_2 & d \end{bmatrix}$

2. $T(0, 0) = (a \cdot 0 + c \cdot 0, b \cdot 0 + d \cdot 0) = (0, 0)$
   $T(1, 0) = (a \cdot 1 + c \cdot 0, b \cdot 1 + d \cdot 0) = (a, b)$
   $T(1, 1) = (a \cdot 1 + c \cdot 1, b \cdot 1 + d \cdot 1) = (a + c, b + d)$
   $T(0, 1) = (a \cdot 0 + c \cdot 1, b \cdot 0 + d \cdot 1) = (c, d)$

3.

a) $T(0, 0) = (0, k \cdot 0 + 0) = (0, 0)$
   $T(1, 0) = (1, k \cdot 1 + 0) = (1, k)$
   $T(1, 1) = (1, k \cdot 1 + 1) = (1, k + 1)$
   $T(0, 1) = (0, 0 \cdot k + 1) = (0, 1)$

b)

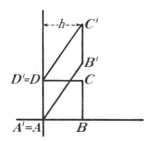

In parallelogram $A'B'C'D'$ with base $A'D'$, the height is AB, so area $= (A'D')(AB) = (AD)(AB) = 1$.

4.

a)

$$T(A) = \begin{bmatrix} 1 & 0 \\ -b/a & 1 \end{bmatrix} \begin{bmatrix} 0 \\ 0 \end{bmatrix} = \begin{bmatrix} 0 \\ 0 \end{bmatrix} = A'$$

$$T(B) = \begin{bmatrix} 1 & 0 \\ -b/a & 1 \end{bmatrix} \begin{bmatrix} a \\ 0 \end{bmatrix} = \begin{bmatrix} a \\ 0 \end{bmatrix} = B'$$

$$T(C) = \begin{bmatrix} 1 & 0 \\ -b/a & 1 \end{bmatrix} \begin{bmatrix} a+c \\ b+d \end{bmatrix} = \begin{bmatrix} a+c \\ -\dfrac{b}{a}(a+c)+b+d \end{bmatrix} = C'$$

$$T(D) = \begin{bmatrix} 1 & 0 \\ -b/a & 1 \end{bmatrix} \begin{bmatrix} c \\ d \end{bmatrix} = \begin{bmatrix} c \\ \dfrac{-bc+ad}{a} \end{bmatrix} = D'$$

b) Area $(A'B'C'D') = (A'B') \cdot$ height

$$= a\left(\frac{-bc+ad}{a}\right)$$

$$= ad - bc$$

5.

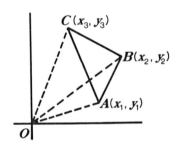

$$\text{area } (\triangle ABC) = \text{area } (\triangle OAB) + \text{area } (\triangle OBC) - \text{area } (\triangle OAC)$$

$$= \frac{1}{2} \det \begin{bmatrix} x_1 & x_2 \\ y_1 & y_2 \end{bmatrix} + \frac{1}{2} \det \begin{bmatrix} x_2 & x_3 \\ y_2 & y_3 \end{bmatrix} - \frac{1}{2} \det \begin{bmatrix} x_1 & x_3 \\ y_1 & y_3 \end{bmatrix}$$

$$= \frac{1}{2} \det \begin{bmatrix} x_1 & x_2 \\ y_1 & y_2 \end{bmatrix} + \frac{1}{2} \det \begin{bmatrix} x_2 & x_3 \\ y_2 & y_3 \end{bmatrix} + \frac{1}{2} \det \begin{bmatrix} x_3 & x \\ y_3 & y \end{bmatrix}$$

If orientation is clockwise,

$$\text{area } (\triangle ABC) = \frac{1}{2} \left| \det \begin{bmatrix} x_1 & x_2 \\ y_1 & y_2 \end{bmatrix} + \det \begin{bmatrix} x_2 & x_3 \\ y_2 & y_3 \end{bmatrix} + \begin{bmatrix} x_3 & x_1 \\ y_3 & y_1 \end{bmatrix} \right|$$

6.

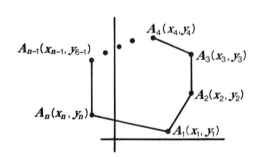

$$\text{area } (A_1 A_2 - A_n) = \text{area } (\triangle A_1 A_2 A_3) + \text{area } (\triangle A_1 A_3 A_4) + \cdots + \text{area } (\triangle A_1 A_{n-1} A_n)$$

$$= \frac{1}{2} \left| \det \begin{bmatrix} x_1 & x_2 \\ y_1 & y_2 \end{bmatrix} + \det \begin{bmatrix} x_2 & x_3 \\ y_2 & y_3 \end{bmatrix} + \det \begin{bmatrix} x_1 & x_3 \\ y_1 & y_3 \end{bmatrix} + \det \begin{bmatrix} x_1 & x_3 \\ y_1 & y_3 \end{bmatrix} + \det \begin{bmatrix} x_1 & x_4 \\ y_1 & y_4 \end{bmatrix} + \det \begin{bmatrix} x_4 & x_1 \\ y_4 & y_1 \end{bmatrix} \right.$$

$$\left. + \cdots + \det \begin{bmatrix} x_1 & x_{n-1} \\ y_1 & y_{n-1} \end{bmatrix} + \det \begin{bmatrix} x_{n-1} & x_n \\ y_{n-1} & y_n \end{bmatrix} + \det \begin{bmatrix} x_n & x_1 \\ y_n & y_1 \end{bmatrix} \right|$$

$$= \frac{1}{2} \left| \det \begin{bmatrix} x_1 & x_2 \\ y_1 & y_2 \end{bmatrix} + \det \begin{bmatrix} x_2 & x_3 \\ y_2 & y_3 \end{bmatrix} + \cdots + \det \begin{bmatrix} x_{n-1} & x_n \\ y_{n-1} & y_n \end{bmatrix} + \det \begin{bmatrix} x_1 & x_n \\ y_1 & y_n \end{bmatrix} \right|$$

Further Investigations

Examine the relationship between the geometry of complex number multiplication and the matrix operations for size transformations and rotations about the origin.

This project allows a geometrical approach to the field of complex numbers. In particular, the development of DeMoivre's theorem is very geometrical and intuitive.

1. $R \circ S = \begin{bmatrix} \cos \theta & -\sin \theta \\ \sin \theta & \cos \theta \end{bmatrix} \begin{bmatrix} k & 0 \\ 0 & k \end{bmatrix} = \begin{bmatrix} k \cos \theta & -k \sin \theta \\ k \sin \theta & k \cos \theta \end{bmatrix}$

$S \circ R = \begin{bmatrix} k & 0 \\ 0 & k \end{bmatrix} \begin{bmatrix} \cos \theta & -\sin \theta \\ \sin \theta & \cos \theta \end{bmatrix} = \begin{bmatrix} k \cos \theta & -k \sin \theta \\ k \sin \theta & k \cos \theta \end{bmatrix}$

Therefore, $R \circ S = S \circ R$.

2. $S \circ R = \begin{bmatrix} k \cos \theta & -k \sin \theta \\ k \sin \theta & k \cos \theta \end{bmatrix}$, $Z = \begin{bmatrix} a & -b \\ b & a \end{bmatrix}$, and $S \circ R = Z$.

Therefore, $a = k \cos \theta$ and $b = k \sin \theta$. Squaring each of these and adding, we have

$$a^2 + b^2 = k^2 \cos^2 \theta + k^2 \sin^2 \theta$$
$$= k^2 (\cos^2 \theta + \sin^2 \theta)$$
$$= k^2 \quad \begin{cases} \text{since } (\cos \theta, \sin \theta) \text{ lies on the unit circle} \\ x^2 + y^2 = 1. \end{cases}$$

Thus, $k = \sqrt{a^2 + b^2}$. Then

$$\cos \theta = \frac{a}{k} = \frac{a}{\sqrt{a^2 + b^2}}$$

$$\sin \theta = \frac{b}{k} = \frac{b}{\sqrt{a^2 + b^2}}$$

3. Let $M_1, M_2, M_3 \in M$, where

$$M_1 = \begin{bmatrix} a_1 & -b_1 \\ b_1 & a_1 \end{bmatrix}, M_2 = \begin{bmatrix} a_2 & -b_2 \\ b_2 & a_2 \end{bmatrix}, \text{ and } M_3 = \begin{bmatrix} a_3 & -b_3 \\ b_3 & a_3 \end{bmatrix}$$

where $a_1, a_2, a_3, b_1, b_2, b_3 \in \mathbb{R}$. Let

$$I = \begin{bmatrix} 1 & 0 \\ 0 & 1 \end{bmatrix} \text{ and } M_0 = \begin{bmatrix} 0 & 0 \\ 0 & 0 \end{bmatrix}.$$

Then show that

$M_1 + M_2 \in M$

$(M_1 + M_2) a00 + M_3 = M_1 + (M_2 + M_3)$

$M_1 + M_2 = M_2 = M_1$

$M_1 + M_0 = M_0 + M_1 = M_1$

$$M_1 + (-M_1) = (-M_1) + M_1 = M_0$$
$$M_1 M_2 \in M$$
$$(M_1 M_2)M_3 = M_1(M_2 M_3)$$
$$M_1 M_2 = M_2 M_1$$
$$M_1 I = I M_1 = M_1$$
$$M_1 M_1^{-1} = M_1^{-1} M_1 = I \text{ for } M_1 \neq M_0$$
$$M_1(M_2 + M_3) = M_1 M_2 + M_1 M_3$$

4.

a) $(a + bi) + (c + di) = (a + c) + (b + d)i$

$$\begin{bmatrix} a & -b \\ b & a \end{bmatrix} + \begin{bmatrix} c & -d \\ d & c \end{bmatrix} = \begin{bmatrix} (a+c) & -(b+d) \\ (b+d) & (a+c) \end{bmatrix}$$

b) $(a + bi)(c + di) = (ac - bd) + (ad + bc)i$

$$\begin{bmatrix} a & -b \\ b & a \end{bmatrix}\begin{bmatrix} c & -d \\ d & c \end{bmatrix} = \begin{bmatrix} ac - bd & -(ad + bc) \\ ad + bc & ac - bd \end{bmatrix}$$

5. $R = \begin{bmatrix} \cos\theta & -\sin\theta \\ \sin\theta & \cos\theta \end{bmatrix}$

a) $R^2 = R_\theta \circ R_\theta = R_{2\theta} = \begin{bmatrix} \cos 2\theta & -\sin 2\theta \\ \sin 2\theta & \cos 2\theta \end{bmatrix}$

b) $R^n = \underbrace{R_\theta \circ \cdots \circ R_\theta}_{n \text{ times}} = R_{n\theta} = \begin{bmatrix} \cos n\theta & -\sin n\theta \\ \sin n\theta & \cos n\theta \end{bmatrix}$

6. $S = \begin{bmatrix} k & 0 \\ 0 & k \end{bmatrix}$

a) $S^2 = \begin{bmatrix} k & 0 \\ 0 & k \end{bmatrix}\begin{bmatrix} k & 0 \\ 0 & k \end{bmatrix} = \begin{bmatrix} k^2 & 0 \\ 0 & k^2 \end{bmatrix}$

b) $S^n = \underbrace{\begin{bmatrix} k & 0 \\ 0 & k \end{bmatrix} \cdots \begin{bmatrix} k & 0 \\ 0 & k \end{bmatrix}}_{n \text{ times}} = \begin{bmatrix} k^n & 0 \\ 0 & k^n \end{bmatrix}$

7.

a) Since $S \circ K = K \circ S$ (problem 1) we have

$$\begin{aligned}
(S \circ K)^2 &= (S \circ K) \circ (S \circ K) \\
&= S \circ (K \circ S) \circ K \\
&= S \circ (S \circ K) \circ K \\
&= S^2 \circ K^2 \\
&= \begin{bmatrix} k^2 & 0 \\ 0 & k^2 \end{bmatrix}\begin{bmatrix} \cos 2\theta & -\sin 2\theta \\ \sin 2\theta & \cos 2\theta \end{bmatrix} \\
&= \begin{bmatrix} k^2 \cos 2\theta & -k^2 \sin 2\theta \\ k^2 \sin 2\theta & k^2 \cos 2\theta \end{bmatrix}
\end{aligned}$$

b) $(S \circ K)^n = S^n \circ K^n$

$$= \begin{bmatrix} k^n & 0 \\ 0 & k^n \end{bmatrix}\begin{bmatrix} \cos n\theta & -\sin n\theta \\ \sin n\theta & \cos n\theta \end{bmatrix}$$

8. Let $z = k(\cos\theta + i \sin(-\theta))$, where $i^2 = -1$

$$Z = \begin{bmatrix} k & 0 \\ 0 & k \end{bmatrix} \begin{bmatrix} \cos\theta & -\sin\theta \\ \sin\theta & \cos\theta \end{bmatrix}$$

$$Z^n = \begin{bmatrix} k^n & 0 \\ 0 & k^n \end{bmatrix} \begin{bmatrix} \cos n\theta & -\sin n\theta \\ \sin n\theta & \cos n\theta \end{bmatrix}$$

$$= \begin{bmatrix} k^n\cos n\theta & -k^n\sin n\theta \\ k^n\sin n\theta & k^n\cos n\theta \end{bmatrix}$$

So

$$z^n = k^n(\cos n\theta + i\sin n\theta)$$
$$z = k(\cos\theta + i\sin\theta)$$

$$Z = \begin{bmatrix} k & 0 \\ 0 & k \end{bmatrix} \begin{bmatrix} \cos\theta & -\sin\theta \\ \sin\theta & \cos\theta \end{bmatrix}$$

$$Z^n = \begin{bmatrix} k^n & 0 \\ 0 & k^n \end{bmatrix} \begin{bmatrix} \cos n\theta & -\sin n\theta \\ \sin n\theta & \cos n\theta \end{bmatrix}$$

$$= \begin{bmatrix} k^n\cos n\theta & -k^2\sin n\theta \\ k^n\sin n\theta & k^2\cos n\theta \end{bmatrix}$$

So

$$z^n = k^n(\cos n\theta + i\sin n\theta)$$

9.

a) $R_0^2 = R_{\theta/2}^2 = R_{\theta/2}\circ R_{\theta/2} = R_{\theta/2+\theta/2} = R_\theta$

$R_1^2 = R_{(\theta+2\pi)/2}^2 = R_{(\theta+2\pi)/2}\, R_{(\theta+2\pi)/2}$

$\quad = R_{\frac{\theta+2\pi}{2}+\frac{\theta+2\pi}{2}}$

$\quad = R_{\theta+2\pi}$

$\quad = R_\theta$

b) $R_m^n = \overbrace{R_{\frac{\theta+2\pi m}{n}}\circ\cdots\circ R_{\frac{\theta+2\pi m}{n}}}^{n\text{ times}}$

$\quad = R_{n\left(\frac{\theta+2\pi m}{n}\right)}$

$\quad = R_{\theta+2\pi m}$

$\quad = R_\theta$

10.

a) $M_0^2 = (S_{\sqrt{k}}\circ R_{\theta/2})^2$

$\quad = S_{\sqrt{k}}^2\circ R_{\theta/2}^2$

$\quad = (S_{\sqrt{k}}\circ S_{\sqrt{k}})\circ(R_{\theta/2}\circ R_{\theta/2})$

$\quad = S_k\circ R_\theta$

$\quad = M$

$M_1^2 = (S_{\sqrt{k}}\circ R_{\frac{\theta+2\pi}{2}})^2$

$\quad = (S_{\sqrt{k}}\circ S_{\sqrt{k}})\circ(R_{\frac{\theta+2\pi}{2}}\circ R_{\frac{\theta+2\pi}{2}})$

$\quad = S_k\circ R_{\theta+2\pi}$

$\quad = S_k\circ R_\theta$

$\quad = M$

b) $M_m^n = (S_{\sqrt[n]{k}}\circ R_{\frac{\theta+2\pi m}{n}})^n$

$\quad = \underbrace{(S_{\sqrt[n]{k}}\circ\cdots\circ S_{\sqrt[n]{k}})}_{n\text{ times}}\circ\underbrace{(R_{\frac{\theta+2\pi m}{n}}\circ\cdots\circ R_{\frac{\theta+2\pi m}{n}})}_{n\text{ times}}$

$\quad = S_k\circ R_{\theta+2\pi m}$

$\quad = S_k\circ R_\theta$

$\quad = M$

11. Let $z_j = \sqrt[n]{k}\left[\cos\left(\dfrac{\theta+2\pi j}{n}\right) + i\sin\left(\dfrac{\theta+2\pi j}{n}\right)\right]$

$z_j^n = (S_{\sqrt[n]{k}})^n\circ(R_{\frac{\theta+2\pi j}{n}})^n$

$\quad = S_k\circ R_{\theta+2\pi j}$

$\quad = S_k\circ R_\theta$

$\quad = z_0$

Statistics

CHESTER PALMER

EVERY day of our lives, people use statistics to try to persuade us to buy some product, vote for some candidate, or adopt some point of view. Such statistics appear in advertisements, news stories, textbooks, and many other places. Because statistics seem precise and impartial, we rarely question their accuracy or the way in which they are presented. Yet statistics are often used incorrectly because of ignorance, and sometimes they are deliberately misused to give a false or one-sided impression. This unit is intended to help you to think critically about the uses of statistics and to avoid being deceived by incorrect or misused statistics. You will not use complex computations in this unit—you can learn those computations in mathematics classes or in a college statistics course—but you will be introduced to many of the ideas that you would use in a more complete study of the subject.

Projects

Project 1

Find at least one example of each of the following kinds of statistics in newspapers, magazines, or books other than statistics books: a sample with a built-in bias, a well-chosen average, a graph or statistic that cannot be properly interpreted because of missing information, a "gee whiz" graph, a semiattached figure, a post hoc fallacy, and a statistic that shows unbelievable precision. In each example, give your teacher a copy of the misleading presentation together with a brief explanation (one or two sentences) of why it is misleading.

Guide: The terminology used above is from Reference 3, the classic presentation of the misuse of statistics. It would be a good idea to read the whole book, which is very short and lots of fun, although you *could* learn enough to complete this project by selective reading. If you want to read more about the misuse of statistics, almost any beginning statistics textbook will have some examples; so do many college textbooks on general mathematics or "liberal arts" mathematics. If you have trouble finding examples of some of the misuses on the list, you might try almost any book that presents large amounts of data, such as Reference 1 or 2.

Project 2

Suppose that you were in charge of a project for a national consumer magazine to determine the frequency of repair for two different brands of television sets. Write a short essay (800–1000 words) describing the importance of sampling in such a study. Explain how you could do such a study using (1) a true experimental design and (2) a quasi-experimental design in which you survey owners who have purchased each brand of set during the past few years. Consider the advantages and disadvantages of each kind of design in terms of accuracy and expense.

Guide: Reference 7 (especially the chapters by Neter, Brown, Battan, Moses and Mosteller, Campbell, and Haight) is the best source of information on the uses and problems of sampling. You can also find discussions of these ideas in any statistics textbook. Although this hypothetical project is a relatively simple one, it is typical of many real-life problems. In serious scientific research, the selection of an approach and the search for an adequate sample are usually much harder, and more controversial, than the analysis and presentation of the results.

Project 3

Complete a project that involves selecting a sample, collecting data, and writing a short report (three or four pages) that describes your procedure and presents your results. The project should involve either the actual collection of real-world data or, if you prefer, the use of a computer to generate data.

Guide: This project is designed to let you practice the ideas of sampling and data presentation on any kind of problem that interests you: flipping coins, rolling dice, counting colors or makes of cars, measuring heights of people or circumferences of trees, studying prices in mail-order catalogs—whatever you like. Or use a computer to simulate what would happen if you did one of these experiments. If you want more ideas, you might check the "Projects" chapter of Reference 6; Reference 4 contains some good situations for computer simulation. Many statistics books suggest projects, and so do many computer manuals. But be sure to check with your teacher *before* you do your project to make sure that it is acceptable; if not, the teacher will probably be able to help you modify it so that it is difficult enough to be interesting but not too hard to be useful. Do your best to pick a good sample, but remember that no sample is ever perfect. When you start worrying about the compromises that you will need to make, you will really be thinking like a statistician—and a scientist.

Further Investigations

If you would like to continue your study of statistics, you can choose any of several directions. If you are interested in learning more about the applications of statistics, you might begin by reading the remaining articles in Reference 7. If you would like to learn more about probability, the mathematical basis for statistics, Reference 4 contains a good treatment. If you would like to know the details of some of the computations statisticians use, any college statistics text would be a good source, especially Reference 8 or 9. (You can understand such texts if you have a good background in algebra.) If you would like to read an entertaining presentation of some more advanced concepts in statistics, you might try Reference 5. Finally, if you would like to investigate still more possibilities for further study, Reference 6 has a good bibliography.

REFERENCES

1. Baum, Paul, and Ernest M. Scheuer. *Statistics Made Relevant: A Casebook of Real Life Examples.* New York: John Wiley & Sons, 1976.
2. Editors of Heron House. *The Book of Numbers.* New York: A & W Publishers, 1978.
3. Huff, Darrell, and Irving Geis. *How to Lie with Statistics.* New York: W. W. Norton & Co., 1954.
4. Kemeny, John G., J. Laurie Snell, and Gerald L. Thompson. *Introduction to Finite Mathematics.* 3d ed. Englewood Cliffs, N.J.: Prentice-Hall, 1974.
5. Kimble, Gregory A. *How to Use (and Misuse) Statistics.* Englewood Cliffs, N.J.: Prentice-Hall, 1978.
6. National Council of Teachers of Mathematics. *Teaching Probability and Statistics.* 1981 Yearbook, edited by Albert P. Shulte. Reston, Va.: The Council, 1981.
7. Tanur, Judith M., Frederick Mosteller, William H. Kruskal, Richard F. Link, Richard S. Pieters, and Gerald R. Rising, eds. *Statistics: A Guide to the Unknown.* San Francisco: Holden-Day, 1972. Also available from NCTM.
8. Triola, Mario F. *Elementary Statistics.* Reading, Mass.: Addison-Wesley Publishing Co., 1980.
9. Walpole, Ronald E. *Elementary Statistical Concepts.* New York: Macmillan, 1976.

Teacher Notes

The wording and content of the first project depend on the availability of the book *How to Lie with Statistics,* by Darrell Huff. There is no real substitute for this book, so you will want to be sure that it is available before encouraging students to attempt this unit. The book has been reissued several times and is often available in public libraries. Project 1 is intended both to alert students to the widespread use of statistics and to identify common misuses. If a student cannot find examples of some of the misinterpretations in any of the suggested sources, you might suggest sensational tabloids like the *National Enquirer* as additional places to look.

You will also want to check on the availability of *Statistics: A Guide to the Unknown,* mentioned in Project 2. There are a number of points that may appear in the essays; it is not expected that any one student will make all these points: Since we cannot trace all television sets produced by a manufacturer, we must sample sets; less obviously, we must also sample users. A true experiment might be to choose certain people shopping for television sets and to give to each of them a Brand A set or a Brand B set, deciding which brand by some random means such as flipping a coin. We should also make sure that the sets are randomly selected from a variety of factory lots. Such an experimental design gives an excellent comparison between brands, since randomization tends to result in well-matched groups of users. But such a design is very expensive, since we can be certain that each shopper acquires the right brand only by giving away the sets. It is much cheaper and simpler to use a quasi-experimental design and survey the people who choose to buy each brand. In this kind of design, since the shoppers decide which brand to buy, we cannot be confident that the groups of users are well matched. For example, because of price and product image, Sony television sets are probably bought mostly by people who are richer and better educated than the people who buy other brands. It seems likely that such people watch less television than others; for that reason, Sonys may be used less than other brands. If so, the fairness of survey comparisons would be seriously compromised. There may also be unknown user factors that affect the repair records of television sets. Only randomization protects us from the biases that may be introduced by such factors. Finally, there is a very subtle psychological point: even if the repair records of the two brands are the same, can we be confident that the two groups of owners will answer the survey with the same degree of accuracy?

Project 3 is deliberately vague because the intent is to allow students to pursue individual interests. Try to make sure that the projects really require sampling. For example, if a student suggests a study of the heights of students in a mathematics class that is small enough to measure everyone, you might suggest enlarging the study to cover all the students in your school. Also be sure that the student understands exactly which group is being sampled: no sample in your community is acceptable for a study of the world-wide average height of adults. Be willing to accept fairly small samples so that the clerical work is not too laborious, but encourage students to think about how best to draw the sample. If you have several students interested in this unit, you might suggest a combined project that could be more extensive than individual projects would be.

The most controversial of the suggestions for further study is the book by Kimble (Reference 5). Kimble is a psychologist, and the book is written for an audience of college students. In particular, it considers a number of experiments on topics such as sexuality, which some students (and parents) might find objectionable. You will need to use some judgment in recommending this book, but it is so well written and entertaining that students who do not object to the topics will almost certainly love it.

Pi and Its History

ROBERT BECHTEL

THE most famous constant (number) in mathematics is pi (π). This number is easily defined from measures of a very common figure of elementary geometry—a circle.

$$\pi = \frac{\text{circumference of a circle}}{\text{diameter of a circle}}$$

The number π has a fascinating history, beginning almost four thousand years ago. Pi leaves a trail of rational number approximations. It appears in metric formulas of geometry as well as in formulas of many other branches of mathematics, including number theory, probability, statistics, and various areas of analysis. As late as 1882, mathematicians puzzled over the question, "What kind of number is pi?" As you might suspect, π is a most interesting number.

The purpose of your work here is to become acquainted with the history of π from the perspectives of its rational approximations, its classification as to type of number, and its appearance in mathematical formulas.

Projects

Project 1

Write a report on what was known about π prior to A.D. 1000. Write at least one paragraph each on the contributions made by these ancient civilizations: the Egyptians (mention the Rhind papyrus), the Babylonians, the Greeks (include Hippocrates and Archimedes), the Chinese, and the (Asian) Indians. Include approximate dates and briefly describe the results concerning π.

Guide: Included in the ancient contributions to knowledge about π are discoveries about relations that exist between measures of parts of a circle as well as various approximations for π. References 1, 2, 3, 5, 6, and 8 are good sources of information.

Project 2

To approximate π, Archimedes used a method of inscribing and circumscribing a circle with regular polygons, continually doubling the number of sides until polygons of 96 sides were obtained, and measuring their perimeters. Pi lies between the two measures. This is called the "classical method."

Make four large drawings to illustrate Archimedes' method. Draw a circle having a diameter of one unit in length and having both an inscribed and a circumscribed equilateral triangle (fig. 1). Use 6-sided, 12-sided, and 24-sided regular polygons in the other three drawings. Using a ruler, approximate the perimeters of the inscribed and circumscribed polygons and record the data in a table.

Fig. 1

Guide: Archimedes used figures with 96 sides to derive the approximation

$$3\frac{10}{71} < \pi < 3\frac{1}{7}.$$

The number 3 1/7 has been called the Archimedean value of π.

Project 3

Complete and extend table 1 for the special sequence of approximations for π.

TABLE 1

	Approximation	Fraction	Average of two consecutive approximations
1st	$4 \cdot (1)$	$4 = \dfrac{4}{1}$	
2d	$4 \cdot (1 - \dfrac{1}{3})$	$\dfrac{8}{3}$	$\dfrac{10}{3} \doteq 3.333$
3d	$4 \cdot (1 - \dfrac{1}{3} + \dfrac{1}{5})$	$\dfrac{52}{15}$	$\dfrac{46}{15} \doteq 3.067$
4th	$4 \cdot (1 - \dfrac{1}{3} + \dfrac{1}{5} - \dfrac{1}{7})$		
5th	$4 \cdot (1 - \dfrac{1}{3} + \dfrac{1}{5} - \dfrac{1}{7} + \dfrac{1}{9})$		
6th	$4 \cdot (1 - \dfrac{1}{3} + \dfrac{1}{5} - \dfrac{1}{7} + \dfrac{1}{9} - \dfrac{1}{11})$		
7th	$4 \cdot (1 - \dfrac{1}{3} + \dfrac{1}{5} - \dfrac{1}{7} + \dfrac{1}{9} - \dfrac{1}{11} + \dfrac{1}{13})$		

Guide: Special sequences called *infinite series* have been used to approximate π. The series below is an example. Table 1 gives the first few approximations for this series.

$$\pi = 4 \cdot (1 - \frac{1}{3} + \frac{1}{5} - \frac{1}{7} + \frac{1}{9} - \frac{1}{11} + \dots)$$

This series was proposed in 1674 by the German mathematician Gottfried Wilhelm von Leibniz (1646–1716) but is attributed to both Leibniz and the Scottish mathematician James Gregory (1638–1675). This sequence converges slowly. However, the simplicity of the infinite series is considered a thing of mathematical beauty.

Project 4

List the approximation sequences developed by the mathematicians François Viète, William Brouncker, and John Wallis. Also indicate the date for each sequence and, if possible, compute the first few numbers in each sequence.

Guide: Many infinite series have been used to produce decimal approximations for π; see Reference 5.

Project 5

Write a paper describing the contributions made by Johann Heinrich Lambert and Ferdinand Lindemann concerning the number π.

Guide: Consider the following information as you describe the contributions made by Lambert and Lindemann:

- The symbol for π is a letter, not a fraction or a decimal.
- A real number that cannot be named by a fraction is an *irrational* number.
- The length of the diagonal of a square having sides each of length 1 is an irrational number, $\sqrt{2}$ (see fig. 2).
- Some irrational numbers are solutions to algebraic equations and hence are called *algebraic* numbers.
- The number $\sqrt{2}$ is a solution for the equation $x^2 = 2$ and is an algebraic number.
- Irrational numbers that are not algebraic are called *transcendental*.

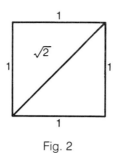

Fig. 2

Your paper should consider whether pi is rational or irrational, then consider whether pi is algebraic or transcendental.

Project 6

List six formulas in which π appears. Show the meaning of each of the letters in each formula. Include the formula from Buffon's needle problem (A.D. 1760) in your list.

Guide: One definition of π is

$$\pi = \frac{\text{circumference of a circle}}{\text{diameter of a circle}}.$$

If c is the circumference and d is the diameter of a circle, then

$$c = \pi \cdot d.$$

This well-known formula is easily derived from the definition. Many formulas with π are found in measurement geometry. Use this source, but also try to find formulas from such other areas as probability, statistics, and number theory. Buffon's needle problem deals with probability (References 3 and 5).

Project 7

Write a paper describing the impact that the computer has had on the computation of decimal approximations for π. Include information about the number of decimal places and the speed at which the computation occurred. List a reference that gives a decimal approximation for π to 1000 places.

Guide: During the nineteenth century decimal approximations for π were calculated with paper and pencil. You may want to compare these efforts with the results obtained in the mid-twentieth century with the aid of the computer; see Reference 4.

Further Investigations

1. Find the approximations for π used on various calculators and computers.

2. If you have access to a computer and can write computer programs, extend the lists of approximations you encountered in Projects 3 and 4.

3. Explore the history of two other famous constants in mathematics, e and G (the ratio of the golden section).

REFERENCES

1. Aaboe, Asger. *Episodes from the Early History of Mathematics.* New York: Random House, 1964.
2. Davis, Philip J. *The Lore of Large Numbers.* New York: Random House, 1961.
3. Eves, Howard. *An Introduction to the History of Mathematics.* Rev. ed. New York: Holt, Rinehart & Winston, 1964.
4. ———. "The Latest about π." *Mathematics Teacher* 55 (1962): 129–30.
5. National Council of Teachers of Mathematics. *Historical Topics for the Mathematics Classroom,* Thirty-first Yearbook of the National Council of Teachers of Mathematics. Washington, D.C.: The Council, 1969.
6. Newman, James R. *The World of Mathematics,* vol. 1. New York: Simon & Schuster, 1956.
7. Read, Cecil B. "Shanks, Pi, and Coincidence." *Mathematics Teacher* 60 (1967): 761–62.
8. Von Baravalle, Herman. "The Number π." *Mathematics Teacher* 60 (1967): 479–87.

Teacher Notes

Project 1

Paragraphs should include information about the following:

- Egyptians (ca. 1650 B.C.)—if one converts to modern terminology, the Egyptians used a value for π equivalent to $4 \cdot (8/9)^2 = 256/81 \doteq 3.1605$ (from the Rhind papyrus).
- Babylonians (1800–1600 B.C.)—used $1/12 \cdot$ (circumference)^2 as the area of a circle, which is equivalent to using 3 as an approximation for π. Other findings show that a correction factor gave 3 1/8 as a better approximation for π.
- Greeks—Hippocrates' (ca. 440 B.C.) "chief result is the proof of the statement that circles are to one another in the ratio of the squares on their diameters. This is equivalent to the discovery of the formula πr^2 for the area of a circle in terms of its radius. It means that a certain number π exists, and is the same for all circles, although his method does not give the actual numerical value of π" (Reference 6, p. 92).

  Archimedes (ca. 240 B.C.)—used a method of inscribed and circumscribed regular polygons to approximate π (see Project 2).
- Chinese—Tsu Ch'ung-chih (ca. A.D. 470) gave 355/113 ($\doteq 3.1415929$) as an approximation for π.
- Indian—Aryabhata (A.D. 510) used the equivalent of $62832/20000 \doteq 3.1416$ as an approximation. Brahmagupta (ca. A.D. 628) used $\sqrt{10}$ ($\doteq 3.162$).
- Middle Ages—the value $\sqrt{10}$ was used extensively as an approximation for π.

Project 2

Students should make large drawings, one on a sheet, of 3, 6, 12, and 24 sides.

Project 3

The averages in the extended table are rounded to the nearest thousandth.

	Approximation	Fraction	Average of two consecutive approximations
1st	$4 \cdot (1)$	$4 = \dfrac{4}{1}$	
			$\dfrac{10}{3} \doteq 3.333$
2d	$4 \cdot (1 - \dfrac{1}{3})$	$\dfrac{8}{3}$	
			$\dfrac{46}{15} \doteq 3.067$
3d	$4 \cdot (1 - \dfrac{1}{3} + \dfrac{1}{5})$	$\dfrac{52}{15}$	
			$\dfrac{334}{105} \doteq 3.181$
4th	$4 \cdot (1 - \dfrac{1}{3} + \dfrac{1}{5} - \dfrac{1}{7})$	$\dfrac{304}{105}$	
			$\dfrac{2946}{945} \doteq 3.117$
5th	$4 \cdot (1 - \dfrac{1}{3} + \dfrac{1}{5} - \dfrac{1}{7} + \dfrac{1}{9})$	$\dfrac{3156}{945}$	
			$\dfrac{32826}{10395} \doteq 3.158$
6th	$4 \cdot (1 - \dfrac{1}{3} + \dfrac{1}{5} - \dfrac{1}{7} + \dfrac{1}{9} - \dfrac{1}{11})$	$\dfrac{30936}{10395}$	
			$\dfrac{422958}{135135} \doteq 3.130$
7th	$4 \cdot (1 - \dfrac{1}{3} + \dfrac{1}{5} - \dfrac{1}{7} + \dfrac{1}{9} - \dfrac{1}{11} + \dfrac{1}{13})$	$\dfrac{443748}{135135}$	

Project 4

- Viète (1592): Formula in Reference 5, p. 151, should be "$\pi/2$."

$$\pi = 2 \cdot \cfrac{1}{\sqrt{\dfrac{1}{2}}} \cdot \cfrac{1}{\sqrt{\dfrac{1}{2} + \dfrac{1}{2}\sqrt{\dfrac{1}{2}}}} \cdot \cfrac{1}{\sqrt{\dfrac{1}{2} + \dfrac{1}{2}\sqrt{\dfrac{1}{2} + \dfrac{1}{2}\sqrt{\dfrac{1}{2}}}}} \cdot \cdot \cdot$$

$$2 \cdot \cfrac{1}{\sqrt{\dfrac{1}{2}}} \doteq 2.8284$$

$$2 \cdot \frac{1}{\sqrt{\frac{1}{2}}} \cdot \frac{1}{\sqrt{\frac{1}{2} + \frac{1}{2}\sqrt{\frac{1}{2}}}} \doteq 3.0615$$

$$2 \cdot \frac{1}{\sqrt{\frac{1}{2}}} \cdot \frac{1}{\sqrt{\frac{1}{2} + \frac{1}{2}\sqrt{\frac{1}{2}}}} \cdot \frac{1}{\sqrt{\frac{1}{2} + \frac{1}{2}\sqrt{\frac{1}{2} + \frac{1}{2}\sqrt{\frac{1}{2}}}}} \doteq 3.1214$$

- Brouncker (1658):

$$\pi = 4 \cdot \cfrac{1}{1 + \cfrac{1^2}{2 + \cfrac{3^2}{2 + \cfrac{5^2}{2 + \cfrac{7^2}{2 + \cdots}}}}}$$

$$4 \cdot \frac{1}{1} = 4$$

$$4 \cdot \cfrac{1}{1 + \cfrac{1}{2}} = \frac{8}{3} \doteq 2.667$$

$$4 \cdot \cfrac{1}{1 + \cfrac{1}{2 + \cfrac{9}{2}}} = \frac{52}{15} \doteq 3.467$$

- Wallis (1658):

$$\pi = 2 \cdot \frac{2}{1} \cdot \frac{2}{3} \cdot \frac{4}{3} \cdot \frac{4}{5} \cdot \frac{6}{5} \cdot \frac{6}{7} \cdot \frac{8}{7} \cdot \frac{8}{9} \cdot \quad \cdots$$

$$2 \cdot \frac{2}{1} = 4$$

$$2 \cdot \frac{2}{1} \cdot \frac{2}{3} = \frac{8}{3} \doteq 2.667$$

$$2 \cdot \frac{2}{1} \cdot \frac{2}{3} \cdot \frac{4}{3} = \frac{32}{9} \doteq 3.556$$

$$2 \cdot \frac{2}{1} \cdot \frac{2}{3} \cdot \frac{4}{3} \cdot \frac{4}{5} = \frac{128}{45} \doteq 2.844$$

Project 5

In 1761 Lambert showed that π is irrational. Lindemann proved in 1882 that π is not an algebraic number and hence is classified as a transcendental number.

Project 6

Formulas for the surface area and the volume of cylinders, cones, and spheres should be included in the list. The formula for the Buffon problem, dropping a needle of length ℓ onto a plane ruled with parallel lines d distance apart ($\ell < d$), is

$$P \text{ (needle falls across one of the lines)} = \frac{2\ell}{\pi \cdot d}.$$

Project 7

An illustration: William Shanks completed computing π to 707 places in 1873 after more than fifteen years of work (Reference 7, p. 761). In 1961 the computation was done on a computer to 100 265 places in eight hours and forty-three minutes (Reference 4). In 1967 an approximation of π to 500 000 decimal places was attained in France on a CDC 6600 computer (Reference 5, p. 153).

Pascal and His Triangle

D. P. JIM PREKEGES

BLAISE PASCAL was a French mathematician of the seventeenth century (1623–1662). He is noted for his work in geometry, especially as it relates to conics. He was also as capable and original in the practical and experimental sciences as in pure geometry. For instance, the first recorded calculating machine was Pascal's invention and was completed in 1642. It was adapted to addition and performed the carrying of tens automatically.

Pascal is also noted for a set of numbers that usually assume a triangular pattern. This triangle of numbers can be developed in a number of ways. The purpose of your work in this unit is to develop the triangle of numbers in two different ways and to find patterns in this unique triangle of numbers.

Projects

Project 1

Examine the life of Blaise Pascal and write a two-page paper noting his experiences and contributions to mathematics (a biographical sketch).

Guide: References 1, 2, and 3 should assist you. Other books related to the history of mathematics should also help.

Project 2

Study the directions in figure 1. Remember that there can be more than one shortest route (more than one route can have the same length). Assume that this figure is a triangle-shaped city. The lines are streets. You live at point A and you wish to visit people at each dot (located at the intersections of the line segments and the ends of the line segments). You do not want to go the same route each time (you must stay on the streets [lines], though), but you do want the *shortest* route each time.

Record at each dot the number of shortest routes you find when you go from dot A to the other dots. Study examples 1 and 2 before you start.

Fig. 1

Example 1

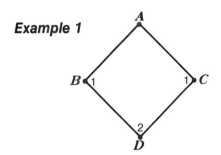

There is one way to go from A to B, so we write a 1 at intersection B. There is one way to go from A to C, so we write a 1 at intersection C. There are two ways to go from A to D, staying on the lines; the paths are ABD and ACD, so we write a 2 at intersection D.

         NCTM Projects to Enrich School Mathematics: Level 3

Example 2

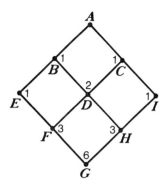

Going from *A* to *F* we have three different shortest paths—*ABEF, ABDF,* and *ACDF*—so we write a 3 at intersection *F*. Going from *A* to *G* we have six different shortest paths—*ABEFG, ABDFG, ABDHG, ACDFG, ACDHG, ACIHG*—so we write a 6 at intersection *G*. There are other paths, but they are not the shortest paths.

Complete recording the number of shortest paths for all of figure 1. Now take the numbers from figure 1 and write them on a clean sheet of paper, keeping every number in exactly the same position.

Guide: After you have studied the directions, the two examples should help to explain the ideas. References 4 and 5 should also be of some assistance.

Project 3

Talk to one of your teachers about probability; you may even want to talk to a high school or college teacher. Investigate the term *equally likely events* and write an explanation for the problem: If two equally likely events occur, the probability for each is 1/2.

Guide: Reference 4, page 82, should assist you.

Project 4

You will use figure 2. Think of each of the following drawings as a pinball machine. Consider each dot to be a peg and consider the line segments to be raised walls that guide the balls. When it says a ball is dropped, that means a ball is started rolling and it hits the first peg. The ball then rolls through the pinball machine until it ends up in a pocket. Your chore is to record the number of balls in each pocket when different-sized machines are used. Study examples 1, 2, and 3 on page 19 before you start.

MACHINE 1
one row of pegs
two balls

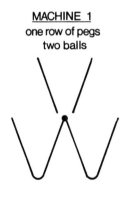

MACHINE 2
two rows of pegs
four balls

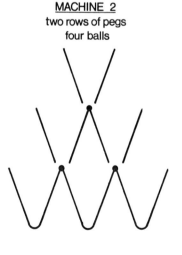

MACHINE 3
three rows of pegs
eight balls

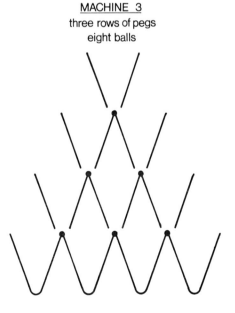

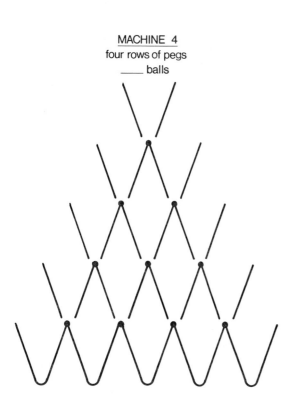

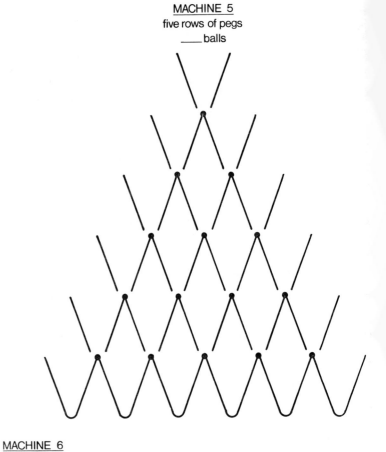

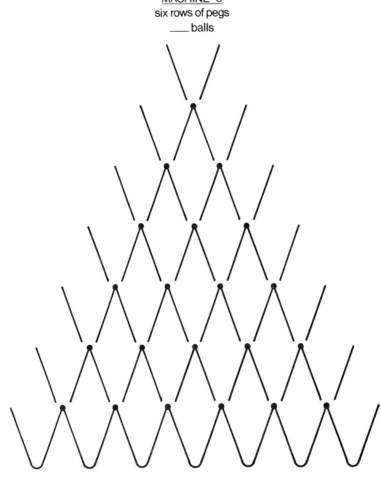

NCTM Projects to Enrich School Mathematics: Level 3

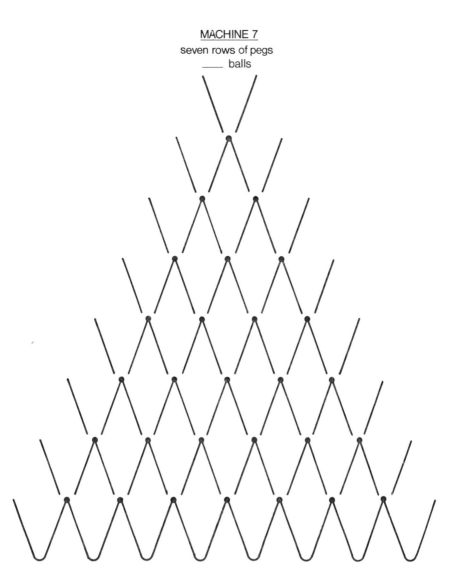

MACHINE 7
seven rows of pegs
____ balls

Fig. 2

Record the numbers in each pocket in figure 2, and then fill in the blanks on the triangular form below as follows.

Machine	Number in each pocket
1	1 1
2	1 2 1
3	1 3 3 1
4	1 4 6 4 1
5	__ __ __ __ __ __
6	__ __ __ __ __ __ __
7	__ __ __ __ __ __ __ __

Compare this triangular array with the one from Project 2. They should be the same. If not, go back and find your error.

Guide: Study the following examples for help.

Example 1. If we drop two balls on the peg, the laws of probability say we can expect one to go to the right and the other to the left—hence one ball in each pocket.

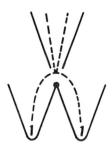

Example 2. This time we will drop four balls on the top peg. They will hit it and bounce left or right. They will then go through the channel, hit another peg, and bounce left or right ending up in the pockets. Again the laws of probability apply: If four balls hit the top peg, we can expect two to bounce each way. Of the two that bounce left, both will hit the next peg, and one will bounce each way. That puts one ball in the left pocket. Of the two that bounce right, both will hit the next peg, and one will bounce left and the other right. That puts one ball in the right pocket and two in the middle pocket.

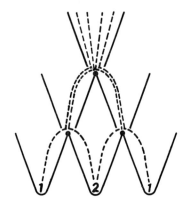

Example 3. Now assume that you had three rows of pegs and four pockets and that you dropped eight balls. How would they end up in the pockets? Determine for yourself that it would be 1, 3, 3, 1.

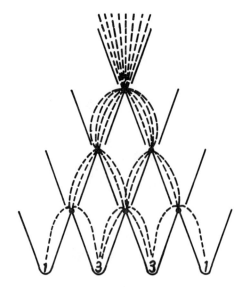

Now assume four rows of pegs and five pockets; determine how many balls you should drop and how they would end up. (1, 4, 6, 4, 1)

Continue for five rows of pegs and six pockets, and so on, until you have completed all of figure 2.

NCTM Projects to Enrich School Mathematics: Level 3

Project 5

By using a discovered pattern, add two more rows of numbers to the triangles that you made in Project 4.

Guide: Examine your triangle of numbers from Project 4. There is a way to get from row four to row five by finding a pattern (for instance, by adding two numbers in row four to get one number in row five). This pattern always holds from one row to the next.

This array, going on forever with a number 1 on top, is known as Pascal's triangle.

Project 6

Find a pattern that enables you to find the sum in any row in Pascal's triangle. List the sum of the tenth row, the twentieth row, and the twenty-third row. You may wish to use a calculator.

Guide: The following chart shows Pascal's triangle and the sums through four rows.

Pascal's triangle	Sum
1	1
1 1	2
1 2 1	4
1 3 3 1	8
.	.
.	.
.	.

Further Investigations

1. Go to the library and find out what is meant by the Fibonacci sequence. Be sure you know the pattern so that you can always get the next number. List the first twelve terms of this sequence and explain how to find the thirteenth term.

Guide: Reference 4, page 50, should assist you.

2. The Fibonacci sequence is hidden in Pascal's triangle. You can find it by summing numbers as you go through the triangle on the diagonals. All diagonal lines are parallel. Find the appropriate diagonals and show that the sum of the numbers on these diagonals produces the Fibonacci sequence.

3. There are many other patterns in Pascal's triangle. For example, the triangular numbers can be found. Find out what is meant by the term *triangular numbers* and then find the triangular numbers in Pascal's triangle. Draw pictures to show how the triangular numbers are developed from triangles.

Guide: References 5 and 6 should assist you.

4. There are other ways to develop Pascal's triangle. You might work out each of the following:

$(a + b)^0 =$

$(a + b)^1 =$

$(a + b)^2 =$

$(a + b)^3 =$

$(a + b)^4 =$

$(a + b)^5 =$

Now examine the coefficients of each of the terms. Remember that a coefficient of 1 is understood. What do they form? Further, examine the order and sum of the exponents of each of the terms. You should find a pattern. You can now use Pascal's triangle and the pattern on exponents to write out the answer to things like $(a + b)^7$, $(a + b)^{10}$, and so on.

5. Pascal and Fermat were friends. They worked on probability. How does Pascal's triangle relate to probability? The concept of combinations is the key and the idea of factorial is necessary to calculate combinations.

6. Draw a hexagon. Now construct (through drawing) the first four hexagonal numbers. Then list the first twelve hexagonal numbers. See Reference 6 for help.

REFERENCES

1. Bell, Eric T. *Men of Mathematics*. New York: Simon & Schuster, 1965.
2. Newman, James R. *The World of Mathematics*. 4 vols. New York: Simon & Schuster, 1956.
3. Smith, David Eugene. *History of Mathematics*. 2 vols. 1923, 1925. Reprint. New York: Dover Publications, 1958.
4. Niven, Ivan. *Mathematics of Choice*. New York: Random House/Singer, 1965.
5. Hughes, Barnabas. *Thinking through Problems*. Palo Alto, Calif.: Creative Publications, 1977.
6. The National Council of Teachers of Mathematics. *Historical Topics for the Mathematics Classroom*. Thirty-first Yearbook. Washington, D.C.: The Council, 1969.

Teacher Notes

Project 1

The biographical sketch should include the following information. Pascal was brought up at home and his education was confined to the study of languages. He was forbidden to read or study any mathematics until he was twelve years old. At that age, Pascal developed a number of geometric properties without the benefit of references; his father then allowed him to begin studying mathematics. He completed his original treatise on conic sections at the age of sixteen. He was eighteen when he built his calculator. At about that same time, he turned his attention to analytic geometry and physics. In 1650 at the age of twenty-seven, he abandoned mathematics to study religion. He died in 1662 at the age of thirty-nine.

Project 2

Figure 1 should look like this.

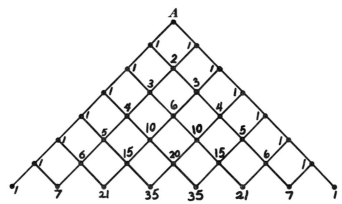

See Project 4 in this section to see how the numbers are arranged.

Project 3

The term *equally likely events* refers to two choices with equal chances of occurring so that we can expect each to occur one half of the time. For example, the chances that a flipped coin will land heads up are equal to its chances of landing tails up. Hence, we expect that it will come up heads half of the time and tails the other half. When a ball hits a peg, its chances of going right are equal to its chances of going left. Hence, we expect it to go right on half of the hits and left on the other half.

Project 4

The last row of each machine should read as follows:

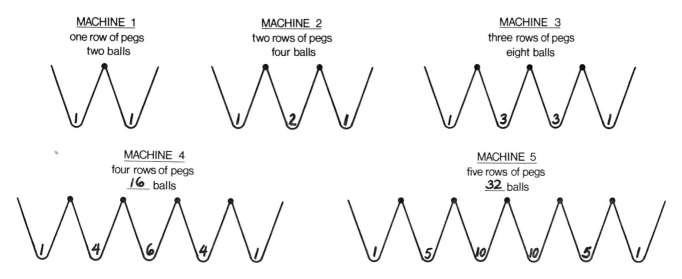

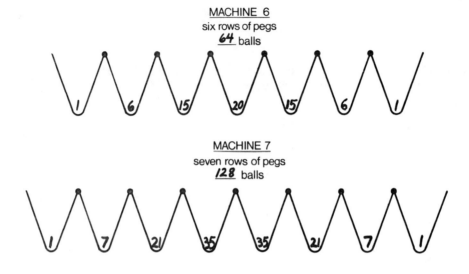

MACHINE 6
six rows of pegs
64 balls

MACHINE 7
seven rows of pegs
128 balls

Students should realize that to get the total number of balls for each machine, they must double the number of balls from the previous machine. The arrangement of recorded numbers will look like this:

```
                    1   1
                  1   2   1
                1   3   3   1
              1   4   6   4   1
            1   5  10  10   5   1
          1   6  15  20  15   6   1
        1   7  21  35  35  21   7   1
```

Project 5

The two additional rows will be

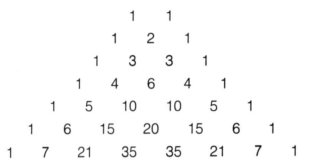

Note how the sums from row eight give row nine: $1 + 8 = 9$, $8 + 28 = 36$, and so on. This sum scheme holds going from any row to the next.

The complete triangle through eleven rows will look as follows:

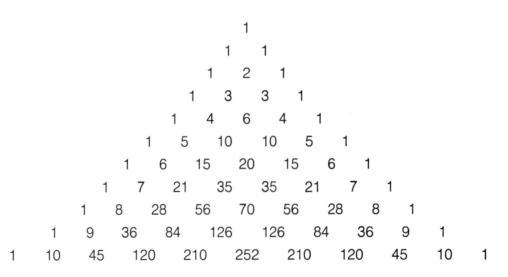

Project 6

The desired pattern is 2^{n-1} where n is the row. Remember $2^0 = 1$, $2^1 = 2$, $2^2 = 4$, $2^3 = 8$, and so on. 2^3 means $2 \times 2 \times 2 = 8$.

For the tenth row, $2^{10-1} = 2^9 = 512$

For the twentieth row, $2^{20-1} = 2^{19} = 524\ 288$

For the twenty-third row, $2^{23-1} = 2^{22} = 4\ 194\ 304$

Further Investigations

1. The Fibonacci sequence is 1, 1, 2, 3, 5, 8, 13, 21, 34, 55, 89, 144, ... Note that the sum of two consecutive terms gives the next number. For example, $5 + 8 = 13$; or, the sum of the fifth and sixth terms gives the seventh term. The next term in the sequence will be $89 + 144$, or 233.

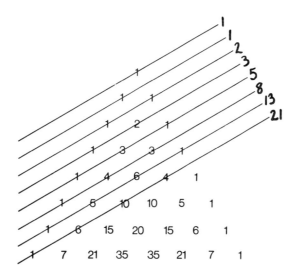

2. Sum the numbers on the drawn diagonals and you get the Fibonacci sequence.

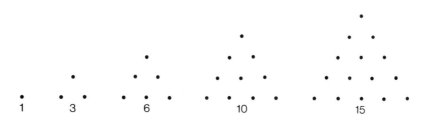

3. Notice this sequence: 1, 3, 6, 10, 15, 21, 28, 36, 45, ... The difference between the next two in the sequence is one more than the previous difference. These numbers exist down the third diagonal.

4. $(a + b)^0 = 1$

$(a + b)^1 = 1a + 1b$

$(a + b)^2 = 1a^2 + 2ab + 1b^2$

$(a + b)^3 = 1a^3 + 3a^2b + 3ab^2 + 1b^3$

$(a + b)^4 = 1a^4 + 4a^3b + 6a^2b^2 + 4ab^3 + 1b^4$

Note that the coefficients form Pascal's triangle. Note further that the powers of *a* descend, whereas the powers of *b* ascend.

$$(a + b)^7 = 1a^7 + 7a^6b + 21a^5b^2 + 35a^4b^3 + 35a^3b^4 + 21a^2b^5 + 7ab^6 + 1b^7$$

For $(a + b)^{10}$ we need the eleventh row from Requirement 5:

| 1 | 10 | 45 | 120 | 210 | 252 | 210 | 120 | 45 | 10 | 1 |

$$(a + b)^{10} = 1a^{10} + 10a^9b + 45a^8b^2 + 120a^7b^3 + 210a^6b^4$$
$$+ 252a^5b^5 + 210a^4b^6 + 120a^3b^7 + 45a^2b^8 + 10ab^9 + 1b^{10}$$

5. The term *combinations* means that of five things, take three at a time. Let the five things be *a*, *b*, *c*, *d*, and *e*. Now, how many combinations of three things are possible at a time?

a,b,c	a,c,d	b,c,d	c,d,e
a,b,d	a,c,e	b,c,e	
a,b,e	a,d,e	b,d,e	

This idea is noted as $\binom{5}{3}$. Mathematically,

$$\binom{5}{3} = \frac{5!}{2!3!} = \frac{5 \cdot 4 \cdot 3 \cdot 2 \cdot 1}{2 \cdot 1 \cdot 3 \cdot 2 \cdot 1} = \frac{20}{2} = 10.$$

Hence,

$$\binom{n}{r} = \frac{n!}{(n - r)!r!}$$

Let's look at some combinations. Note that 0! is defined as 1; 1! is also defined as 1.

$$\binom{4}{0} = \frac{4!}{4!0!} = 1 \qquad \binom{4}{1} = \frac{4!}{3!1!} = 4 \qquad \binom{4}{2} = \frac{4!}{2!2!} = \frac{4 \cdot 3 \cdot 2 \cdot 1}{2 \cdot 1 \cdot 2 \cdot 1} = 6$$

$$\binom{4}{3} = \frac{4!}{1!3!} = 4 \qquad \binom{4}{4} = \frac{4!}{0!4!} = 1$$

$$1 = \binom{4}{0}, \quad 4 = \binom{4}{1}, \quad 6 = \binom{4}{2}, \quad 4 = \binom{4}{3}, \quad 1 = \binom{4}{4}$$

This is one row in Pascal's triangle. The pattern holds for all rows.

6.

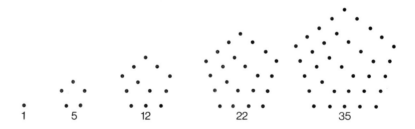

1, 5, 12, 22, 35, 51, 70, 92, 117, 145, 176, 210